THE ELDER WITHIN

The Source of Mature Masculinity

Terry Jones MA, M.Ed.

THE ELDER WITHIN

*The Source of
Mature Masculinity*

Terry Jones MA, M.Ed.

BookPartners, Inc.
Wilsonville, Oregon

Library of Congress Cataloging-in-Publication Data

Jones, Terry, 1940-
    The elder within : the source of mature masculinity / Terry Jones.
    p. cm.
    Includes bibliographical references.
    ISBN 1-58151-088-8 (trade paper : alk. paper)

    1. Aged men—Psychology. 2. Aged men—Conduct of life. 3. Masculinity.
I. Title.

HQ1061 .J53 2001
305.31—dc21

                                                                2001025785

Copyright © 2001 by Terry Jones
All rights reserved
Printed in U.S.A.

Cover art used by permission:
The Voyage of Life: Old Age
© 1971 Thomas Cole
Ailsa Mellon Bruce Fund, photograph © 2001 Board of Trustees
National Gallery of Art, Washington.

Cover design by Richard Ferguson
Text design by Heidi Bay

This book may not be reproduced in whole or in part, by
Electronic or any other means which exist or may yet be
developed, without permission of:

BookPartners, Inc.
P.O. Box 922
Wilsonville, OR 97070

To the Magnificent Seven,

Linda
Jason
Caleb
Nicole
Amy
Joshua
Jeremy

CONTENTS

Teacher

PREFACE

When I first learned about elders and their opportunities and responsibilities, I wanted to meet some of them. At the end of each of the first five chapters is a quote from and a vignette about five men I have known who express elder energy. They are hard to find so I went in search of them. I listed what I felt were qualities of an elder, wrote them down and carried them in my wallet. I went from person to person asking if anyone knew men who fit that description. Over the time I wrote this book I identified over a dozen men deserving of the title of "elder." The fallibility of these men struck me right away. An elder is not, I discovered, an example of a perfect man, or even a completely balanced one. I have gained increasing hope, therefore, that most people could, over time, become more elder-like. Any man committed to sharing his wisdom and remaining accessible could. Any man willing to let go of his biases about aging and confront his mortality could become an elder. Any man willing to forgive those who harmed him and release the wasted energy used for holding grudges can embrace eldership. Any man can seek out the young to sponsor them and make their spiritual journey a little easier.

My search for elders developed into a passion. I began to do research on eldership. I discovered that men throughout early history evolved into a role called *elder* in the second half of life. The role of the elder differed considerably from what we call today, the *elderly*. The elderly today are a relatively small number of older people who fail to celebrate their life accomplishments, and remain angry and hurt over harm done to them long ago by people they refuse to forgive. The elderly live in fear of life and death, or they long for life to end. The elderly older person of today scares the young and reinforces the bias we grow up with about aging.

i

However, an elder was, for thousands of years, shown extraordinary deference by the community in which the elder was a senior member. The second half of life was a time not of retirement but of service. The elder celebrated long life experience by becoming a human resource for the young who hungered for initiation into adulthood, the training of a master craftsman or wisdom's blessing.

The reason this book is about male elders is that I am very interested in my own masculinity. I wrote it because I am looking at just how grown-up I am at age sixty. The other reason is that women are much better at embracing elder energy. A number of women have been my teachers on this subject. I became a seminar leader for the Spiritual Eldering Institute, one of the only national organizations that addresses the concept of elder directly. Most of the people teaching for the institute, and most of the people showing up to be taught, are women. I am a certified spiritual director, the significance of which will become clearer to the reader as you discover the spiritual emphasis of this book. The leader of the school that trained me and the majority of the others seeking this training were women.

I wrote this book, therefore, because I am discovering something new in my life. Throughout my life I have written down thoughts on new life challenges. When, 25—30 years ago, my wife and I were birthing our children, I became enamored with the role of expectant fathers. I self-published a handbook for expectant fathers. When I did my research in graduate school for my thesis, I came across a little known Japanese-American, Kanaye Nagasawa, and eventually co-authored a book about his life. Paul Kadota and I published the book in Japan. When I opened one of the first firms devoted to selling counseling services to business and industry, I wrote and published a handbook for employers entitled, *Employee Assistance Programs in Industry.*

Now as I embrace the experience of being a grandfather, a retired mental health consultant and spiritual director, I have an uncontrollable need to deepen spiritually, to understand how to harvest my life experience, and increasingly be accessible to my family and my community. Thus, this book.

As I have delved into the concept of "elder," I have been both fed and left hungry. I am fed by the hopeful potential of eldering as a way of being in the second half of life. I am hungry for the acceptance of the idea of eldering. To most people of my father's generation, it is too tiring to consider a celebration of one's wisdom and long life experience. To the young in this culture, the idea of utilizing older people as mentors is unfamiliar. Those inclined to eldering will have to prove themselves to the young. To many women, a book about men as elders sounds like a dangerous call to patriarchy. It is not. Eldering makes men's wisdom available to the young, and to the community the men were too busy to serve earlier.

Venturing into the world of elder is a paradox. It is a new idea for our culture based on an ancient tradition from most other cultures. Our founding fathers understood the role of the loving and balanced older people they called elders. But, shortly after fighting for independence, laying the groundwork for the North American version of the Industrial Era and creating a land of the free and a home for the brave, the value of elder energy diminished with the increasing pace of progress. I have attempted, therefore, to modernize the concept of eldering for the twenty-first century. The reader will now judge how successful I have been.

INTRODUCTION

As I approached the age of fifty, my interests began to shift away from a quest for power, away from molding my children, away from competition and away from "doing" for its own sake. The reality of midlife caused me to consider my mortality. My maternal grandfather lived to age fifty-five. My paternal, to age sixty. My father, who is eighty at this writing, will probably live to see ninety. At midlife I was feeling as good physically as I ever had. Would I live to be 100? What was my role going to be in this long second half of life?

I had spent the better part of half a century striving for success, ensuring that I provided for my family, being a dutiful husband and effective father to my six children. My work required competing with others for position and power. In the course of work, I had ignored my health, gained too much weight, and I had chronic back strain. My risk for heart disease increased with elevated cholesterol and blood pressure. I had not allowed time to build friendships. My lifestyle was constructed on assumptions common to most men. These included the belief that I had to attain my professional and financial success before I got too old. I assumed that my credibility as a man, as provider and protector, as a source of wisdom would begin to diminish once my hair turned gray. I bought into the American perception of older people as a doddering, powerless lot. There are exceptions. We admire Bob Hope and still consider Sophia Loren sexy. Yet for every Tony Bennett, whose age has only added to his icon status, there are a million senior citizens that will never be celebrities. Society merely considers them old.

At age fifty, things began to happen to me that led me to ask myself about my potency, image and value. Was I entering a stage of life where I was to be seen as just an old man? I was left with a void, an emptiness inside that I needed to fill. I wanted balance—physically, intellectually, emotionally and spiritually. At the same time my balance was rocked by three major life events: the marriage of my youngest daughter, the discovery of a new passion and the subsequent impact my new passion had on my business.

When my daughter married, she seemed fulfilled in the way I was when I married her mother thirty years earlier. She accomplished it by making a commitment to her soul mate. I was learning for the first time how hard it was to let go of a child and celebrate at the same time. This was the end of my love affair with my daughter as a twosome. I fell in love with her husband, too, thus creating a threesome. This was for me, both a new start and a kind of death—a message about mortality. Shortly after the wedding she graduated from college, the family gathered together at commencement to hear her graduation talk. She ended her talk by announcing who were the most influential people in her life. While she mentioned my name, when she got to her new husband, she described him as "the person who completed her!" When I realized that I couldn't have that position in her life, the grieving that began at her wedding took a deeper dip.

The next "aha" hit me when I realized I was not as energized by my work as I had always been. I had founded a business and begun building my career about thirty years earlier. At age fifty, however, I found myself depending more and more on my staff to maintain the day-to-day management of the company. Almost overnight I had lost passion for the work. We were all caught off guard. To my surprise, what became painfully clear was that I was not as essential to the business's success as I had been. I had hired and built a staff of creative and energetic people who brought youthful vigor and imagination to the operation of the company.

I began a search for a new passion. When the search began I spent about a year letting go of the passion I had for my profession. This was another little death, a transition that made it possible for me to pursue my search but, nevertheless, a transition that required grieving, a letting go once again. I began writing this book then and forming a dream about men in the second half of life.

My drive for power, influence and control shifted into a quieter, less aggressive energy. As I began a study of men I found that this shift was common to most after mid-life. I found myself wanting to inspire younger people by employing rational and hopeful encouragement. I wanted less to lead, to make decisions or to attain more status. My parenting approach had shifted away from "in your face" and more toward advocacy from a greater distance. My children were becoming adults and needed me within reach but no longer needed their mother and me to define the railings and boundaries. Performing, executing, transacting, discharging, achieving and working had been core to my use of energy most of my adult life. I began to feel a hunger for just being present, contemplation and celebration of life. This all spoke to me about spiritual hunger.

My new passion, the search for the elder within is the subject of this book. This is a search both in the world and inside myself. I imagine American men as they enter retirement taking on roles such as mentor, mediator, and a source of blessing. Most American men, however, don't have models for how to utilize the expanded life span that is available to us nowadays. We lose ourselves in work for most of our adult lives. Like our fathers before us, we have been emotionally distant from our children. We are unskilled in nurturing our spirit while at the same time sensing that we are cut off from our soul. About the same time the changes I mentioned above were occurring, I got involved in the Men's Movement. I wanted to understand what masculinity meant in the second half of life. I participated in ritualized weekend workshops and ongoing men's groups. Like me, men of all ages shared a hunger for spiritual and emotional growth. Many of us missed the nurturing only a father can bring because our fathers were unskilled in connecting to us emotionally. It was in these men's gatherings that I was reminded about the *elder*. The older men present for the weekends came to be known as the *elders*. They tried to fill a vacuum left after two centuries of diminishing credibility for elders. The elders of pre-industrial communities had been available to the young. As newly initiated elders, we did our best to play the role of grandfather, mentor or sage, but men and boys need the real thing.

The Elder Within presents and illustrates the relationship between the acceptance of the responsibility of eldership and the recovery of men from damage done to their souls in recent history. In the eighteenth century men became detached from family and community as they moved from farm to factory. Competing for jobs, men forgot the joy of collaboration. In order to survive they learned how to assert power in the workplace. Then they returned to their homes and allowed their power to darken the nature of fatherhood.

In pre-industrial times, men utilized archetypal warrior power to protect their homes and families. Later, the urbanized male used the same power to compete for position. We guarded our economic vulnerability by creating an emotional armor that, because of its rigidity, led to an even greater personal vulnerability. Today we decry abuse by men who beat their wives, perpetuate violence and discriminate against minority citizens and women. These are not mature men. In this book we celebrate mature men who express *mature masculine* qualities.

It has become difficult, however, for our culture to celebrate the rich roles based on the *mature masculine*. These include protector, teacher of cultural tradition, adventurer, problem solver, father, provider and impassioned lover in spiritual union with his mate. Ancient civilizations celebrated the uniqueness of both genders. They often related the two to the ongoing dance of natural phenomena: earth and sky, land and sea, rain and soil. When we modernized the world with machines, we revised the historical roles of men and women. We separated men from the home and the land, and left women overwhelmed with parenting and the care of the home. Next, we caused confusion by redefining "masculine" and "feminine." We have forgotten that masculine and feminine are descriptors of expression and behaviors resulting from energy within our psyche. For example, males are not the only aggressive people and sensitive doesn't mean female. The masculine expression called assertiveness is an energetic approach made by a man or a woman. "Emotional people" are those of both genders who are intimate and expressive of what they feel. Both genders have access to the individual and collective energies of masculinity and femininity.

In this book, I treat the transition in gender roles in the same way that social scientists consider most change with its four stages: shock, resistance, exploration, and adaptation. The Industrial Revolution of the eighteenth and nineteenth centuries was the *shock* stage for the historical expression of mature masculinity. In the twentieth century women led us through decades of *resistance* to the devastation of *immature masculinity.* Women attacked the "feminine mystique" and the inclination of some men to dispossess women of their rights to equality.

The assault of feminism and many men's acquiescence to its demands has ground down the assertiveness of too many men who feel confused about their power. There has, for too long, been a silence about the increasing destruction of diversity of mature archetypal masculine traits.

The twenty-first century could incorporate the *exploration* and *adaptation* stages of change to a modern definition of mature masculinity. With mentoring, men could again learn how to access the ancient archetypes of generative masculinity from within themselves. In this book, the reader will review the historical patterns of instinctual mature masculinity available in the unconscious. With advocacy and good modeling, the twenty-first century male could access these unconscious and latent resources. The immature male has remained a boy in chaos not by choice, but because no one has shown him the way to grow. Increasing patterns of fatherlessness and increasing numbers of voluntary out-of-wedlock births have left both boys and girls without father advocacy. The prejudice in this culture about aging, combined with the increasing divorce rate, has separated children from their grandparents. With industrialization came an increasing lack of respect for older mentors who could not teach survival in factories that did not exist when they were learning a trade. Only the young could survive under the demands of the factory. With immigration and the separation of older people from their ancestral homes, North American men turned increasingly to their peers for support and training. Boys grew up without the initiation to manhood that the young received in the older rural community. Older men used to teach younger men their skills, model male expression and offered the magic of presence that came with being in the energy field of a male mentor.

This book is an exploration into the potential of eldership, the second half of life adventure, in modeling mature masculinity. You will discover that *elder* means being a "steward of life," both human life and the life of our planet. It does not mean that an elder has complete balance, but he seeks to affirm life. The elder fosters consensus rather than conflict and competition. He energizes himself through use of the tools of wisdom: meditation, contemplation, and listening. He accepts his mortality and honors his body, which he knows is in depletion. With this knowledge he models taking care of himself, an uncommon North American male trait. Most of all, the man who embraces eldership makes himself available to younger men, to the family and to the community. He has confidence in the fruits of his long life of experience and wants to seed the future by sharing with the young.

In chapter one you will read about the power of the elder's blessing, the affirmation that says he is making an active commitment to assist you in obtaining your dream. Any man inclined to serve society in the second half of life is embracing eldership. Because few elder models exist, western men assume that the second half of life means resting, declining in health and becoming useless. An elder's depletion is only physical however. He addresses old age by reaping what he has sown rather than whining about reduced strength. In this chapter, I will review the decline of the elder's credibility over the past few centuries and consider the concept of eldership as a victim of progress. You will read about the potential and meaning of mentoring, and how "mentor" is a new role that came out of the industrial era as a substitute for elder.

Chapter two reviews masculine expression throughout history and the impact of industrialization on mature masculinity. The facts about the impoverishment of men are reviewed, including the startling fact that the life expectancy of men and women was equal until the nineteenth century. Men are dying younger because of immaturity, because they have lost touch with their personal power, and because they have lost touch with the healthy expression of the traditional roles of protector, provider and teacher. This is a hard chapter to read because the dark side of men has led to abuse of women and children, an increasing tendency to desert the family, a dangerous level of exploitation of the earth's resources and worst of all, a deadness in our spirit.

Chapter three is a review of the history of eldership. You will read about ancient elders, like those of Moses' time, primitive elders found in indigenous cultures, and the conversion from generative eldership to the exploitation of patriarchy. Out of the Christian era came a number of holy men who modeled some aspects of eldership. However, they lost the trust of younger men by getting caught up in a hunger for power in their leadership of organized churches. Some consideration is given to the wise man and the sage as two older versions of elders. The Renaissance is reviewed because of the emphasis on youth and cultural renewal. Society had less appreciation for eldership in the sixteenth century than at any other time in history. The oppressive gerontacracy of more recent history is considered in chapter three as a major cause for emigration to the New World.

In chapter four, I begin to speculate about the potential of utilizing archetypes of masculinity in world history as a base for a redefined mature masculinity that works in the twenty-first century. It is in this chapter that I introduce the concepts of psychoanalyst Carl Jung. He called his historical masculine and feminine models *archetypes*. We can find them in written myth and stories, and in psychic energy in the collective unconscious. We consider four archetypes of masculinity: King, Lover, Warrior and Magician. Each archetype has a positive and negative energy. Understanding and taking charge of both the positive energy, and what Jung called *shadow* energy, challenges the mature masculine man. Another challenge is converting the way we play traditional male roles into twenty-first century application. A third challenge of mature masculinity is to integrate both masculine and feminine traits into the expression of self.

In chapters five and six, the reader will find information on how to become elder-like. In chapter five, I offer three processes that encourage growth into eldership. The first embraces eldership as a stage of human development. "Growing up" gets you there. Next, I offer a design for an initiation into the role of elder. Initiation is the capacity to learn something new and demonstrate it to someone else. This process takes no less than six months to complete and takes the initiate through the three stages of most rites of passage: separation, threshold and incorporation. The third and most complex process is to do the intellectual, psychological and spiritual work necessary to grow into eldership.

Chapter six is called "Action Elderhood," not because the world needs aged activists but because eldership is known to the world by its works. The elder is a spiritual person who believes that he exists for a reason. His search for the reason is what I call the spiritual journey. This journey takes the action elder where he can serve others, empower others, and bless his family. At the same time he honors the reality that each day brings him closer to death than he was when he was an "action youth." Action elderhood moves the heart more than the legs. The elder gleans the energy he needs from his contemplative activity. The older he gets, the more he becomes acquainted with his spiritual center. The actions suggested in this chapter are separated into three categories: provider, protector and teacher. Action elderhood is the route to how mature men can play these roles in the twenty-first century.

Chapter I

ELDERS

And now begins the story
Where men are touched,
Deeply by older men
Missed for so long.
Yet a place in the heart
Still hungry, still ready.

The second half of a man's life can be an adventure in eldership: a life of stewardship instead of exploitation; of fostering consensus instead of competition; of spiritual expression instead of a lust for power; of mentoring rather than directing. *Eldership* is wisdom in an active state utilized on behalf of others. Older men and women express eldership with a spiritual journey leading them to intellectual, emotional, physical and spiritual balance. There are older men who are not "traditional" in the expression of their masculinity. They are balanced in their expression of strength, intelligence and feeling. They are elders. An elder is not necessarily always very old. An elder has, throughout history, been a person who celebrates life and energizes others with his passion. He can accurately assess his strengths and skill because he knows his limitations. An elder is often a wise man, a sage. Elders have their faults but carry themselves well despite the fact that they are human. Elders operate from their heart, their center.

The loving and wise mentor or grandfather of history is scarce today. Three historical forces have contributed to the rejection of the mantle of *eldership* among older men: the move of people in the eighteenth century away from rural life to an urban-industrial existence, the soul-wrenching impact of two world wars, and the emigration from the Old World to the frontier of North America. Western men evolved into people who could manage the factories of the Industrial Era. They were, at the same time, both the perpetrators and victims of two highly mechanized and deadly wars. Men moved into the frontier of the New World almost entirely without the support of grandfathers, master craftsmen and other elders.

One Elder

Doug was the manager of human resources in a large company. He supervised Ivy, a woman who coordinated benefits for employees. She was known as the "iron lady" because of her stern and aggressive interpersonal style. Those of us who knew the "iron lady" watched her evolution into a more gracious adult as she allowed Doug to influence her. The mere experience of being around Doug caused her to change. One notable day, Doug went to her after she had explained to an employee, rationally but impatiently, how the employee's health insurance didn't cover marriage counseling. Doug said to her, "Ivy, the employee was revealing to you that he had marital problems. He was looking for information, which you gave him. However, he could have been seeking help."

"Are you saying I should be his marriage counselor?" Ivy responded defensively.

"You are the benefits manager in a department of *human resources*. You have knowledge about resources that he doesn't have. You could both listen briefly and refer him." Doug said.

"I didn't think of that. You're right. I moved too quickly." Ivy conceded.

"A person with the knowledge you have can be a wonderful resource," said Doug. "Ivy, each time a person comes to you, try to leave them with a little more than they had when they walked in," Doug said.

Doug is a man who can tap elder energy in himself when needed. Ivy trusted him because she felt safe with Doug. He had his faults but Ivy had worked with him long enough that she had come to believe he was a mentor and neither a competitor nor a bureaucrat wanting only to wield his power. Ivy went on to become a very good human resource manager herself. She was stirred by Doug's natural ability to reach into the hearts of other people. Elders like Doug access a balance of masculine energies from the human soul. If Ivy "grows up" to become an elder herself, it will be in part because she was energized and motivated by Doug.

A Centered Man

A centered man is patient, loving and available to others. He is not in need of power. Community, cooperation and consensus stir these men. They are men who have been shown *extraordinary deference* by those who come to know them. Extraordinary deference is polite regard, an appreciative yielding shown to an elder. Traditional masculine attributes including competition, patriarchy and emotional control don't appeal to an elder because these processes don't nurture the soul.

Elders know that assertiveness can be motivating and invigorating. They speak their minds and are generative, meaning they have a life-giving energy others can absorb. The generative man facilitates growth and procreation. The elder is a conservationist in his admiration of life. Elders are husbandmen. Husbandmen are driven by archetypal hard-wiring to improve and maintain a stable relationship to their family and to the Earth. The ancient and universal archetype of the mature male suggests a pride that comes from the conscious care of his own health, as well as family and stewardship of the land and its limited resources.

Elders believe the role of adults is to facilitate creativity in the young, not teach the patterns of the past. This often leads to mentoring, and mentoring is time consuming. It leaves less time for recreation, self-indulgence, building a base of power or collecting things and creating wealth. Elders, in their wisdom, sense that they are caretakers and that their vitality depends on a personal shift from self to community. A man is an elder if people are liberated, empowered and healed by his presence.

Affirmation by Elders

When my oldest son reached the age of eighteen years, I felt for the first time ever a desire to release him. I had been aware only at an intellectual level that I would need to let him go someday. It felt like he was ready not so much to be an adult but rather to be honored as a boy who was ready to consider adulthood. My wife and I planned a ceremony that would have the purpose of blessing my son and showing our respect for his individuality.

On the day of his "blessing ceremony," we gathered in our home with all our children. We played music we thought conveyed the feeling of honor and love. My wife and I wore clothes that my son would consider unique and special for his day. Each of the six of us, in turn, told our eldest son what we appreciated about him, including his uniqueness, and his beauty. Each of us closed our brief remarks with a spontaneous hug. As the oldest male member of our nuclear family, I acted as the family's representative and presented my son with a gift that symbolized his maturity and the family's confidence that he was becoming a man. His name is Caleb but he had created a fantasy name for himself, Draxx. Caleb was an avid reader of myth and loved J.R.R. Tolkein. Our gift to him was a full-sized sword of the kind warriors in Tolkein's stories might carry. We had the name, Draxx, engraved on the blade. Caleb breathlessly took the sword from my hands and held it like it was a delicate piece of art. He was speechless but we all knew we had hit pay dirt with that sword.

With each of our five children, my wife and I have been drawn over and over again to ceremonially let each child go and to encourage his or her adulthood. My wife and I feel our children have selected each of us as the elders of their family—their nuclear family. Other special, trustworthy adults in our extended family also serve as elders for our children. The blessing ceremony is an endorsement, an affirmation of each child that only a trusted elder can offer.

The people in the community who bless others include ministers, coaches, teachers and even some employers. I believe they are describing elders. If you observe closely, the "blessing," the affirmation that these trusted elders offer, has at least five parts:

- Touch
- Special words
- An expression of appreciation to the blessed
- Referencing for the other a dream or special future
- An active commitment to the other to help them realize their future, their dream[1]

An elder affirms people through this process of unconditional positive regard. This affirmation plays a major role in the growth of those blessed. You can see this in ceremonies like the laying-on-of-hands in the ordination of priesthood in Mormon churches or in the laying-on-of-the-sword in the bestowing of knighthood. The one blessed, ordained and honored is believed to have moved from one spiritual realm to a higher one. He grows. He is initiated. The blessing is performed by an elder who is respected by the community such as the church community or the community of kings and knights. The blessing is offered in *sacred space*—holy ground created when people are both seen and heard, recognized, admired and affirmed by another. If the person blessed is ready emotionally, intellectually, physically and spiritually, the affirmation can change a person's life forever.

Thus, the process of blessing, of initiation, has four aspects:

- A community's endorsement
- Sacred space
- An elder's affirmation
- Readiness and absorption of the blessing by the blessed

The blessing of an elder can come from teachers, master craftsmen, fathers, and mentors. It usually does not come from bishops and kings in the lives of most men.

A Father's Blessing

My father gave me a shotgun when I turned thirteen. He took me pheasant, duck and pigeon hunting. Giving me the gun was his best try at saying to me, "You are becoming a man." The act of presenting me with the shotgun had the potential of blessing. He could have taught me gun safety, for example. He didn't initiate me into knowing about the great danger of holding a loaded gun. He didn't honor my fear of the gun. He could have taken me aside, listened to my questions and made the moment a memorable experience. Men have yearned for fathers who could take us by the arm and lead us into the world of other men. My dad was not well enough trained by his father. My father didn't play the role of elder in making of me a hunter, but rather attempted to bless me by trusting me with the responsibility of owning a shotgun. The gun remains today one of my most treasured possessions even though I never chose to become a hunter.

Initiation

The philosopher Joseph Campbell, psychologist Erik Erikson and educator Jean Piaget proposed schematics for stages of growth. In the process of initiation, a man makes movement up through a stage of growth. Initiation is a fundamental element of movement from a man stage to the next stage. Initiation is a ceremonial admission into a group or society. For the initiate, the ceremony is the kick-off to a new beginning, an introduction. It requires instruction by those sponsoring the initiate in the fundamentals or principles of the new group or society.

In the United States, men's gatherings have experimented with initiation for a number of years. Through organized weekend meetings or by building small communities in ongoing men's groups, men have been looking for something they missed in the course of growing up. The sponsors of these gatherings and workshops seek to create an environment that facilitates healing and personal growth through the use of small group exercises, mock experiences that facilitate grieving and initiation rituals copied from African and American Indian traditions and drumming. They try to replace the elements of initiation the men missed as they were growing up.

Anthropologist Arnold Van Gennep studied the ceremonies of various cultures that accompanied mens' passages from one part of their life to another. He coined the phrase *rites of passage*. These rites, he said, honored the reality that "life itself means to separate and to be reunited, to change form and... to die and to be reborn.... And there are always new thresholds to cross: the thresholds of summer and winter, of a season or a year, of a month or a night; the thresholds of birth, adolescence, maturity, and old age; the threshold of death..."²

Many men are hungry to become mature males. They want to experience a soulful life expression, express emotion more fully, and embody sexual passion rather than exploit women sexually. They want to recover from addictions and find consensual alternatives to competition. The gatherings provide respite and growth opportunities for the men attending. What many have come for, however, is initiation. They want to move up to the higher stages of being a mature person.

The fourth element of initiation, the hunger and readiness of men is often evident at men's gatherings. The two elements of initiation that aren't present, however, are true community and its representative elder. The weekend gatherings provide a newly formed, temporary community with an individual or individuals assigned the role of "elder for the weekend" or what is commonly called the *ritual elder*. Community can't be created in a weekend. The communities that know a person well enough to celebrate his passages from a man developmental level to another take years to form. They include family, church and sometimes hometown neighborhoods. Others are fraternal lodges, professional associations and labor organizations. In each of these communities an elder is a man who has built personal credibility over an extended period of time. The ritual elder of weekend workshops can only be a symbol of the community endorsed elder.

Many have found that family is the best community in which to grow through the stages of life. Some mothers and fathers understand the importance of initiation. Prophet Kahlil Gibran said in *The Prophet*:

> Your children are not your children. They are the sons and daughters of life's longing for itself. They come through you but not from you. And though they are with you yet they belong not to you... You are the bows from which your children as living arrows are sent forth. Let your bending in the Archer's hand be for gladness; For even as He loves the arrow that flies, so He loves also the bow that is stable.³

Not all parents have the ability, knowledge and the passion for facilitating their children's growth. Often people lack a church community. A neighborhood can keep changing as new families move in and out. In today's fast changing world, people don't put down many roots. Professional associations often lack depth and there has been a decreasing membership in fraternal organizations. College fraternities don't usually get to know each "brother" well enough to qualify as a body of people who understand personal needs for advocacy and initiation in the process of growing up.

By the time I met my wife, she and I had formed separate communities of friends that knew and loved us. Both my family and my personal friends endorsed my marriage to Linda. They wanted for me the joy and stability marriage would bring. To bestow a blessing, we selected a priest. He had the credentials to marry us but was not a member of my community. The people who spoke for our community and who were intimate enough with my wife and I were our parents. They were the elders in this ceremony. They were the people most passionately involved with us to see us, hear us and release us. My parents saw a role for themselves in our marriage ceremony, but they didn't think of themselves as facilitators of an initiation. They didn't know my need for their endorsement, their sponsorship of my growth. This sponsorship was better understood by elders of pre-modern cultures.

Eldership

A few years ago, a good friend said to me, "You have no choice about it, you are an elder." He was reacting to my reluctance to accept leadership in a spiritual community of which he and I were co-founders. I wanted to simply participate in the group and not be burdened with the role of board member. He saw that the group was seeking leadership and he admired my ability to facilitate groups and to operate a successful business. Joseph Campbell wrote, "The first requirement of any society is that its adult membership should realize and represent the fact it is they who constitute its life and being… [and to] establish in the [young] a system of sentiments that will be appropriate to the society in which he is to live, and on which that society itself must depend for its existence."[4]

The elder, unlike the "elderly," knows he owes advocacy to young people. I intend to redefine the word *elderly.* The elderly complain about aging or spend their retirement separating themselves from the young. The elder continues to deepen his experience of living. The elderly remain angry about experiences that hurt them throughout their life. They have not yet forgiven. While the young move from "obscurity into prominence, from present to future, the elder moves back home, into the past, and toward the deeper and more fundamental strata of human experience."[5] The elderly don't celebrate life. They are just trying to get through it. What many are hungering for is a quality in older people called *eldership.* One writer approached this idea by describing what he calls "elderhood" as a "state of consciousness that arises in the context of physiological aging… [where] the psyche issues a call for us to engage in life completion, a process that involves specific tasks, such as coming to terms with our mortality, healing our relationships, enjoying our achievements and leaving a legacy for the future."[6]

The archetypal elder has been the same force in most cultures over most all of time. An archetype is an ancient model for a role that has survived time. Some writers refer to the archetypal "elder within" when discussing the energy from the psyche that energizes those who express eldership. "Within each person awaits the figure of the elder—a promise and a challenge."[7] Just as the instincts seem to account for recurrent behavior patterns in man, so the archetypes seem to account for recurrent psychic patterns. Psychic patterns are expressions of your psyche. The psyche is all of the human being, which is not physical. The psyche includes the conscious and unconscious elements of the human personality. When a man taps the energy of the "elder within," the following are available to him:

- Balance in our expression of strength, celebration, intellect and feeling
- Knowledge of our faults, our shadow
- An expression of self principally from our center, our soul
- Patience and a desire to be available to others
- An awareness of our personal strength

- A sage-like love for consensus and community
- A expression of wisdom that leads to being shown extraordinary
- Deference by the community
- A hunger to share the world with women and children: the opposite of patriarchy
- A drive for conservation and a passion for the Earth and its survival
- Assertive energy that invigorates and energizes but is not dangerous to others
- Generativity
- Husbandman energy: driven by a passion for the best possible life for men and the beauty of the Earth
- Stewardship energy of the Earth, of people
- A desire to take care of ourselves and take pride in our good health
- Knowledge that we are caretakers whose vitality depends on a personal shift from self to community
- A personal force that empowers others when they are in your presence
- A hunger to introduce the meaning of life to the young

Elders have a "detached concern with life...in the face of death itself," according to psychologist Eric Erikson. Wisdom, Erikson felt, "maintains and learns to convey the integrity of experience..."[8] Elders are men and women of wisdom. Eldership is wisdom in an active state. Wisdom is enlightenment, insight and a high degree of learning. The elder is aware of the need to pass on one's knowledge and to pass on the responsibility of stewardship of man and the Earth to the young.

My Search

The average person has met few elders. They either have gone underground or are simply few in number. As my hunger to meet them grew, I began a search for those who expressed eldership in 1995. In my wallet, I carry a card that describes an elder. He is someone who:

- Is seasoned, and a source of life-giving energy
- Knows his limitations and is skillful
- Has an unconquerable spirit
- Is knowledgeable, aware and filled with insight
- Is intuitive, passionate, spiritual and sensuous

I began asking people if they knew a man of wisdom. I told people I was seeking out elders so that I could interview them. I read the card out loud. In the past few years I have found my way to a number of men who expressed eldership. How important these men are! They are a resource for young people to access. Throughout this book I will be quoting from a number of them. None of them is a Mahatma Gandhi, a Winston Churchill or a Martin Luther King, Jr. They have not needed to risk their life for a cause. None of them has written a book or gained media attention in any way. Their greatness stems from their willingness to share their wisdom and help heal, to express their humor and their soulful spirit.

The older men I have met so far had one thing in common: they were in touch with their spiritual life. They were as close to being "balanced" men as I have met: balanced emotionally, physically, intellectually and spiritually. Some were more concerned than others with their physical health. Some were more expressive emotionally. They all struck me as intelligent—wise men feel that way. They varied in their focus on intellect. What was true to all is that they were patient, at peace with themselves, tolerant. They are generative, loving men in whose presence I feel empowered.

To address life from the center, the spirit, does not mean a person need be perfect. These elders are not gods. My reverence for them suggests they are godlike when, in fact, they are wonderfully human. They admit openly that they struggle with the challenges of the ego and their humanness. Three are recovering alcoholics. Two of them are workaholics.

One feels he drinks too much. One man declares that his manner is too often childlike and he knows he doesn't fit many people's view of a grown-up. And another admits that his stressful approach to life has caused him significant health problems.

Elders and the Aged Lose Credibility

The men's movement in America has moved me deeply. My search has been for male elders because of my dream for male liberatio—liberation from an impoverishment of soul and self that goes back centuries. There is a hunger among men for fathers and mentors that is as old as the time of impoverishment that began when the extended family began to disintegrate. Women today have an average of 1.8 children in their lifetime. Before 1860, families consisted of over five people. This was primarily a nuclear family with an occasional grandparent. The pre-Industrial Era village contained numerous extended family menders.[9]

The fathers, master craftsmen and other male mentors such as uncles and friends of the extended family left the agrarian home about 200 years ago. They went away to work in the cities to feed their families. The work they went to do was meaningless, was not of the Earth. This move, this enclosure of men away from the home, began the destruction of the Earth that is so apparent today. The pride of the elders, the spirit and joy of the elders, and the husbandry by the elders began to suffer when the men left home. Two other historical events added to the diminution of the elders the immigration from Europe to America; and the Second World War.

An uncontrolled movement of people from all world cultures into the United States occurred in the nineteenth century. It was the young and hardy who took on this adventure. Most of the older people remained in their native countries. The American culture from about 1900 on was made up of the children of immigrants. Absent were the elders who were still in their home country. The offspring of the immigrants were forced to create a culture based largely on the observation of their peers, who offered more practical models than those of the few elders who did immigrate. The past of the older people was inaccessible to them. For the young, the future was difficult to see as their own. The ancestors of the Eskimos, for example, who historically had come from an oriental culture in the Old World, also lacked the knowledge and depth and variety of experience needed to thrive in the New World. Most of their elders remained in their natural surroundings in Asia. Both the New Americans and the old Eskimos lacked the depth, therefore, to adapt, to grow to maturity. The founding "fathers" in this country were in fact "founding sons, rebellious sons, refugees from patriarchal gerontocracy. They had run from the stifling tradition of being monitored by the repulsive, chiding, gossiping elders in claustrophobic villages."[10]

World War II stripped away more of what was left of our father's abilities to pass on to us whatever sense of manhood remained. Bill Kauth, co-founder of the Mankind Project, one of the largest and most successful men's training programs, said, "Our dads took on the awesome mission of WWII with great courage, and they were wounded, deep inside. They were in the first fully automated war. The sense of genuine "warriorship" was grotesquely distorted or absent. These were men (like their fathers) doing meaningless work who were operating cold machines that delivered death miles away or miles below. And, the final blow, the climactic culmination of WWII, was the atomic vaporization of thousands of men, women and children."[11]

When my father was in his seventies he asked me if there was more that he could have done to help me grow up when I was in my teens. It is my belief that he was not capable of giving more than what he gave due in large part to his WWII experience. The war damaged his spirit. He had been used as a part of a deadly war machine. For the remainder of his life he was diminished in his ability to experience intimacy.

Industrialization and the breakup of the extended family, immigration and the devastation of the human soul in WWII separated old men from the young. In pre-modern times, before the eighteenth century, young men discovered manhood by being in close proximity to older men: fathers; master craftsmen; grandfathers; uncles and older friends of the family who were living in the same village. Older men needn't be elders, in the finest sense, to model maleness. Some of the older males exhibited eldership but all men, mature or not, left behind a pathway for the young to assess as their own.

In America today, old people are denigrated. Many find people over sixty years of age to be noxious, in the way, bothersome, weak and lacking in intelligence. The distance we feel between older people and the young is a uniquely Western problem. We try to drown out any intuition we might have about aging through high stress activity, competition, entertainment, sexual experiences, alcohol abuse and other obsessive habits. Old people remind us of our mortality. Our judgment is that death is a mistake and we try to avoid it as long as possible. Anticipating death, however, is guaranteed to deepen a person's appreciation of life. Our denigration of older people is more an expression of our fear of aging than a statement about the value of older people.

Sigmund Freud theorized that two forces drive human experience: libido, the life instinct and thanatos, the death instinct. Freud, the "father of psychiatry," believed life included a struggle between these two forces. "Libido surges with vitality, seeking pleasure and continuity of experience. Thanatos longs to return to an inanimate state of quiescence devoid of all striving and conflict."[12] In *The Prophet* Gibran wrote, "Your fear of death is but the trembling of the shepherd when he stands before the King whose hand is to be laid upon him in honor. Is the shepherd not joyful beneath his trembling that he shall wear the mark of the King? Yet is he not more mindful of his trembling?"[13] When we access the death instinct we can be energized in a way that is comparable to the charge we get from libido. Accepting mortality, we are more inclined to celebrate the time we have left and get the most out of the present moment.

The way we think about elders is lost in how we view the elderly. Our fear of death and our consequent desire to stay young and stay around young people gets in the way of seeking out elders. Our language overflows with words and phrases we use to separate ourselves from old people: "relic of the past, old relic, out-of-date, not-with-it, old fossil, obsolete, over-the-hill, old fogey, old codger, old crock, crotchety, decrepit, doddering, gray beard, senile, outmoded, little old man/lady, wizened, wrinkled, superannuated, archaic, second childhood, dotage, past their prime, having one foot in the grave, antiquated, toothless, old biddy."[14] When the United States was formed in 1776, the founding fathers turned to the young for energy and their hunger for individual expression. The

"New Americans" wanted to avoid "the mistakes and excesses that had reduced the Mother Country into an "old, wrinkled, withered, worn-out hag!" Interesting it was, however, that they chose the bald eagle as our national bird. If this means some ambivalence prevailed, it probably resulted from the young American' wish that the old were more dependable.

The young Americans of the eighteenth century displayed an "uneasiness with decorum, gentility and the propriety one expects from old people."[15] A fear of old age and old people was rampant. By the end of the nineteenth century historian Frederick Turner was appealing to Americans to cherish one's youth. "The older they grow, the more they must reverence the dreams of their youth," he said.[16] In pre-modern times the elder was venerated. The Puritans saw in old people the image of God…. "and when His majesty and eternity are set forth in Scripture, it is with white hair."[17] The old were seen by these early Americans as standing on the boundary between the "natural and unnatural worlds." The assumption made in pre-modern times was that the old were wiser because of accumulated experience. In communities where literacy was less common, it was the older people who provided not only education but also a connection to the past. Their memory was the unrecorded history of the people.

One early writer said, "Though your infirmities be never so many and great, you have peculiar honor that is twisted with your infirmity, for it is called the Crown of Age."[18] The old were expected to be dignified in that they wore the Crown of Old Age. This led, incidentally, to the expectation that they would live with restraint. A minister of the eighteenth century wrote that the old were "expected to be sober, grave, temperate, sound in faith, charity and patience…. They were to be always a living example of the good old way for the public."[19] So, not only were the old respected but they apparently had to work at maintaining that respect. There was an assumption in the community, shared by older people, that being old earned a man a heightened level of respect. In those days it was seldom questioned whether an old person was truly wise. When the elderly were fewer in number, perhaps it was easier to value them as a resource. "In the world of high fertility and high mortality, where the population was very young and the odds against surviving to a ripe old age were great, respect for age was enhanced by its comparative rarity."[20]

The Status of the Old

There are a number of other factors that seem to affect the status of old people in a culture. The foremost has always been property ownership. The influence of the landed citizen has been significant ever since people stopped their nomadic wandering and held onto "things." The two most energetic classes of people in American history, however, were the pioneer and the entrepreneur. These two risk-takers were capable of confronting new horizons without the wise old men to guide them. In a New World, young people with new ideas and lots of energy accomplish a great deal on their own. The pioneer found his own land. He had less need for inherited land and, therefore, was less influenced by the older people from whom he might inherit land. The entrepreneur built businesses and accumulated wealth in a community of young and hardy people. The old people who owned land were left behind.

The next most significant factor determining the status of old people after possession of land is the possession of strategic knowledge. To be "strategic" the knowledge would need to be applicable, for example, in the management of a person's economy, the raising of children or in the maintenance of their health. The old people who immigrated were a resource in their homeland "strategically" but much less in the New World. Another factor determining status has always been the predominant modes and styles of economic productivity.[21] Once again, the old in the New World were unskilled because what they had learned about economy and survival was in another, older culture.

Before the Industrial Era, families were clustered closely together. In the seventeenth century the village commons were the primary social units of England. In this system the peasantry, at least, "comprised a village community of shareholders who utilized the majority of the land on a collective basis." By the eighteenth century, millions of craftsmen and artisans in England and throughout Europe were beginning to see the "degradation of their labor and the undermining of their families through the displacement of handicrafts by machines."[22] The era of machines drew the men away from the village commons and into the new way of life that began the breakdown of the extended family. Old men could not compete for the new industrial jobs. Respect for them by younger men, therefore, began to wane. So, the fourth factor of status, an ethic of mutual dependence, began to loose its potency. The older people became less and less necessary to the survival of the family.

Yet another factor of significance is "the importance of received tradition especially religious ones." Received tradition could be defined as the inherited transmission, from generation to generation, of customs, practices and knowledge.[23] Initiation, discussed earlier in this chapter, is a ceremonial admission into a group or society. Of the four elements of initiation (i.e., community, sacred space, the elder, readiness of initiate) the elder's blessing comes to mind when a person received tradition. What has happened in modern times is that elders have become less visible and ritual initiation has occurred less often. Tradition is not being "received" as readily as it was in pre-modern, pre-industrial times. Consider this statement by Russian philosopher G.I. Gurdjieff:

> One day I read an article stating that among the ruins of Babylon some tablets with inscriptions had been found which scholars were certain were no less than four thousand years old. The magazine also printed the inscriptions and the deciphered text—it was the legend of the hero of Gilgamesh.
>
> When I realized that here was that same legend which I had so often heard as a child from my father, and particularly when I read in this text the 21st song of the legend in almost the same form of exposition as in the songs and tales of my father, I experienced such an inner excitement that it was as if my whole future destiny depended on all this. And I was struck by the fact, that this legend had been handed down by men (such as my father) from generation to generation for thousands of years, and yet had reached our day almost unchanged.[24]

Survival of the Fittest

Veneration of the older citizen in colonial America created continuity, stability, permanence and order in the society. The privileges of old age were apparent even in the arrangement of permanent seating in the meeting houses. These community halls were used regularly and were a core aspect of maintaining a sense of community in early America. But, one by one, the governing committees of the meeting houses changed the seating arrangements. The change began in the late eighteenth century and it only took a generation to complete the transition. Rather than assigning seats by age and respect, the committees sold the seats to the highest bidder. The shift from a "pluralistic system of stratification to a unitary system" was based largely on wealth.[25] A stratified society with the old highly represented at the top was coming to a close.

Adam Smith's *Wealth of Nations* was published in 1776. Smith's philosophy laid the foundation for the *free-market doctrine*. Smith taught that society could become wealthy by following your self-interest and honoring the laws of supply and demand. In 1859 came Charles Darwin's Origin of Species whose dictate was that the strongest and most fit survived in the evolution of all species. Men and women of the industrial era read Darwin to suggest that survival at any price was a natural behavior in the market place. This also suggested that the youngest, richest and most competitive should be preeminent. Around 1800, the authority of age began to be undermined and at the same time the direction of age bias began to be reversed. The doctrine of profit and the ethic of competition were new and unique to Western societies.

Men began to move toward the cities and away from the village community of elders, craftsmen and fellow farmers on common land. Joint work and shared roles in farming and craftsmanship waned in favor of the more competitive world of industrial production. Men were becoming a collection of competitors for scarce jobs. The change in older men's relationship to younger men was becoming apparent. Older men stopped seeing themselves as responsible for teaching and mentoring the young. The young were seen as a threat. The young were becoming more capable of taking over the jobs and they lost respect for the older and less competitive men.

In ancient eastern philosophy such as that found in India, the final and highest stage of life was what the Hindu calls the *sannyasan ashrama*. This was the time a person left their property and family and lived in poverty with a commitment to self-realization and service to society. In China, Taoism taught that in old age a man is set free from the prison of his possessions. The Taoist felt that a person is thus promoted to the rank of living spirit. Although modern people of India and China are questioning the utility of these ancient philosophies, it was western men who led the way off the land, out of the soul and into the world of competition for wealth that, in a twist of fate, has robbed men of independence, security, liberty and birthrights.

The movement away from family and the land was a turning point for male and female gender roles. Women were forced to stay home, watch the children, do the washing and generally maintain some connection to the community in which they lived. Men were away from home while at work. They had to compete for jobs and do work that was meaningless except for the income produced. Work began to mean long hours performing rote tasks away from a person's family for income earned, not from the sale of his crafts but from the sale of his time and energy.

Working for money, for gain, is only as old as the eighteenth century. The village commons had an economy based on subsistence, handicrafts and the sharing of land. In medieval Christian society, people were condemned for attempting to gain profit from the sale of goods or the loaning of money. The central principle of most pre-modern cultures was gift-giving. Anthropologist Bronislaw Malinowski found in his work studying old cultures that financial gain never acted as an "impulse to work under the original native condition."[26] The Industrial era concept of working for income alone not only moved men out of the village but separated them from their reason to celebrate their creativity and survival skills.

Fathers living in the twentieth century were emotionally detached from their family and were away from home a great deal. This poem written in 1868 depicts the family condition of the family with a father who worked for wages:

Father is Coming.

The clock is on the stroke of six,
The father's work is done.
Sweep up the hearth and tend the fire,
And put the kettle on.

The wild night-wind is blowing cold.
'Tis dreary crossing o'er the world.
He's crossing o'er the world apace,
He's stronger than the storm;
He does not feel the cold, not he,
His heart, it is warm:
For father's heart is stout and true,
As ever human bosom knew...
Nay, do not close the shutters child;
For along the land,
The little window looks,
And he can see it shining plain.
I've heard him say he loves to mark
The cheerful firelight through the dark.

Hark! Hark! I hear his footsteps now:
He's through the garden gate.

Run, little Bess, and open the door,
And do not let him wait.
Shout, baby, shout! And clap thy hands,
For father on the threshold stands.

Elders as Victims of Progress

Grandfathers living today came from a generation of men who were among the first victims of the Machine Age, which began around 1850. These men gave up their usable property by leaving the villages and the farms for work in the factories. They lost economic independence by depending on wages. "They lost spiritual independence as their fear of starvation and joblessness made them subservient to their bosses."[27] The soul is alive when one has spiritual independence. Nurturing the soul requires listening to the wee small voice inside us. The work-a-day world places a heavy demand on that part of us that is desperate, fearful. This takes us away from our spiritual center and leaves our soul hungry. In his landmark book, *The Hazards of Being Male,* Herb Goldberg speaks about the bind a man is in vocationally:

> In order to meet the definition of success, he must continue to be upwardly mobile, to strive for promotions and to take on greater and greater responsibility. In the process, however, he often has to give up doing that which he once did best, what originally attracted him to his work, and which gave him the deepest satisfactions. As he advances, he will also find it increasingly more difficult to relate to former coworkers and others who were once his friends. If he contents himself with continuing to do the thing he does best and enjoys most and avoids promotion, he may be seen as unsuccessful and may also make his own future vulnerable to those who will pass him by....[28]

In the race for more promotions, more power and money, men are motivated more by fear and desperation than by satisfaction and qualities that nurture the soul. A man who confronts life motivated only by competition for power and money is not acting out of his soul. The soul is the "you" that is immortal. The ego, which is not immortal, usually acts out of fear and is driven to seek power. Following only the energy of the ego, a person willingly sacrifices intimacy and, thereby lacks wisdom.

The soul is a positive, goal-directed force that emanates from the center of your being. When a man reviews the nature of eldership, he finds soulful expression. The loss of connection to his spirit—his soul—interferes with eldership.

Because of the bias we have toward older people, the elder of the Western world reaches the second half of life lacking confidence in his wisdom. Coupled with the resulting lack of pride is a lack of clarity about how to be an elder. One writer talks about the increasing number of people living to old age as a "new class of the old." He says they "are utterly untaught, their education is completely neglected, their part is unwritten."[29] Another writer states that our community of potential elders has an unprecedented high level of physical health but no models for how to live a full life. "The time at which old age begins is ill defined…nowhere do we find any initiation ceremonies" for your entrance into elderhood.[30] The quotes above are from writers who are talking about elders in the West. In many cultures outside the western world, becoming an elder is natural to older people.

The new class of the old, which people might call the "fifth age" of man, is a phenomena of the last three generations in the west. It has resulted from longer life spans. My grandfather didn't notice it. My father sees it but has no model for it. At age sixty, I am entering the fifth age and there are some advocates who suggest some rules.

Initiation into into elderhood, for example, begins with a voluntary relinquishment of specific personal status and executive authority. "All that is retained is an advisory influence, but even so no specific rulings would be given."[31] The *advisory influence* is only possible if a man accepts the role of elder. This automatically implies sharing wisdom with the young.

Mentoring

As mentioned above, myths and tales from pre-modern times contain standards of behavior for elders called archetypes. According to many scholars, the archetype of an elder found in old stories includes seven tasks that confront people from mid-life forward:

- Dealing with the specter of decline
- Self-confrontation and self-reformation
- Shifting from a youthful preoccupation with things to an empathetic understanding of human nature

- Breaking free of personal ambition and dreams, which dominate youth
- Liberating yourself from socially compromising community mores
- The reclamation of wonder and delight in life
- The seventh and most challenging task is said to be "taking the transcendental inspirations of later life and using them to help the next generation."[32]

Providing counsel and inspiring youth is spiritual stuff! The passion to mentor the young can be doused by a fear-driven hunger for survival—a legacy of the Industrial era.

A few decades into this century we began to hear a new use of the term *mentor.* During the Western world's revolution against conformity in the 1960's, we heard that mentoring meant something like eldership. At the foundation of this redefinition of mentoring you could find a hint of the hunger for initiation that is prominent in the men's movement today. Initiating relationships with mentors began to fill the 200 year-old void.

A good mentor is a mixture of father and good friend. But unlike both fathers and good friends, the new mentor of the twenty-first century is a transitional figure. He invites a young man into the adult world by acting as guide, teacher, and sponsor. A mentor represents not only skill, knowledge, virtue and accomplishment but also love.

The mentor is not a parent. In early adulthood a young man shifts from being a child to being an adult in a peer relation with other adults. The mentor is a mixture of peer and father. A peer by himself cannot model the advanced level toward which the younger man is moving. On the other hand, if the mentor is too fatherlike, it is hard for him and the "mentee" to overcome the generation difference and move toward the goal of peer relationship.

The soulful expression of effective mentoring comes as the mentor gives his "blessing" to the mentee and honors the dreams of the younger man. The dreams provide a vague sense of what it is like to be true to self in the adult world. One researcher studied the concept of what he called the *Dream*. He said the Dream has the quality of a vision, an imagined possibility that generates excitement and vitality.[33] Although examples of a young man's Dream surface in mythology and fairy tales, they seldom show up in studies on psychological development. Whether called the Dream, fantasy or a plan for the future, the young man is more likely to reach his life's goals if his Dream has been endorsed, blessed by an older person he trusts and admires. A young man has the task of giving his Dream definition, then discovering ways to live it out.

Developing through the stages of human growth is a more complete process if a man structures his life around a Dream. If the Dream is not satisfied, it may fade away. The man's sense of aliveness and purpose will fade also. As a young adult grows into adulthood, he must separate from his mother and his father. He needs, therefore, to form relationships with adults who will facilitate his work in realizing the Dream. Both a special female relationship and a mentor relationship are of great importance to the task of breaking away from parents and forming an adult life.

Finding mentors is difficult for most men. In pre-modern times, boys worked side-by-side with fathers, grandfathers and other extended family. If a young man wanted to seek out other older men, there were craftsmen, clergy and men of other occupations within a short distance. The smaller communities of the village commons and rural towns were comprised of small gatherings of people mutually dependent upon one another. When a man was ready to exhibit eldership in the form of mentoring, it was easy for the young people to find him. The pre-modern elder was rarely anonymous.

Even though the modern workplace emphasizes teamwork, seldom do workers form mentoring relationships. Even colleges and other schools seem to not foster quality mentoring connections. Many older person/ younger person connections have an aspect of mentorship in them, but true mentoring is not a simple passing on of intelligence. "In a 'good enough' mentoring relationship, the young man feels admiration, respect, appreciation, gratitude and love for a mentor."[34] A mentor may teach. He may sponsor, using his influence to cause a special opportunity to be revealed to the mentee. A mentor is a host sometimes, introducing the young man to a group which he wants to join or learn about. Mentoring is often like being a guide, showing someone the "ropes" and advising on faulty choices and creative choices. Counseling is a mentoring function. To the mentee, the true mentor is a model, an archetype in the flesh.

The most developmentally crucial role of the mentor is his support for realization of the Dream. To love another person is to vibrate with their aspirations, their hopes and their joys. To facilitate the realization of another man's Dream is to bless him. To bless him someone need share the Dream and its possibilities, and feel the charge it causes in the young man's psyche. A man must take time to be in tune with the center of another person. People who love take time because they are patient and willing to stand by until the one loved "gets it."

It wasn't until Hermann Hesse's *Siddartha* was a grown man that he met his greatest mentor, Vasudeva, the ferryman. The rich man turned buddha, Guatama Siddartha, was seeking enlightenment. From the humble and poor Vasudeva, Siddartha first learned that his mentor was not a teacher. "I am not a learned man, I do not know how to talk or think, " said Vasudeva to Siddartha. "I only know how to listen and be devout, otherwise I have learned nothing." Siddartha experienced the joy of having "a listener who could be absorbed in his own life, his own strivings, his own sorrows."[35] As others with mentors have discovered, Siddartha found that a mentor is trusting and trustworthy, noble, trusts in a universe larger than himself, is empathetic and affirms life in those for whom he is a model.

Philosopher Martin Buber wrote in his poem, *The Disciple:*

The gray hand of the storm lay over both.
The Master's hair bore a black glow.
Enveloped and rocked to sleep in dumb suffering,
Was the face of the disciple, pale and kind.

"The gray hand of the storm" describes the dark passage through fear of the unknown, the unexplored areas of life. Both the "Master" and the "disciple" are victims of the storm, the only certain difference being that the "Master" has been through more of the passages than has the "disciple." Buber continues,

> *The way was rocky. Lightning and mountain fire*
> *Zigzagged around them like trembling branches.*
> *The boy's step grew weak and ever more timid,*
> *The old man walked as always, straight and firmly.*
>
> *The blue eyes gazed dreaming into his own,*
> *And through the narrow cheeks beat the shame,*
> *The mouth was set as from repressed weeping,*
> *The great longing of a child came.*

This part has the Master in shame with his mouth "set as from repressed weeping."

Shame is a sense of unworthiness. The older person here feels an obligation to mentor but experiences the fear of not being good enough. And the older man's own longing to be innocent, like a child, rises up. Buber closes with:

> *Then the master spoke.*
>
> *From much wandering*
> *I took the golden might of the one truth:*
> *If you can be your own, never be another's."*
> *And silently the boy walked in the night.*[36]

The only thing that the Master assured the boy was his willingness to be present. His devotion to the task of mentoring was so great he felt unworthy, not arrogant. The mentor's wisdom was to assure the boy that the two of them were equals. This devotion is love in action.

Mentoring is a relatively new word. It was created to fill a vacuum formed when the fathers left home. Fathers and grandfathers are far more than mentors when they act in the fullness of their role. They love like brothers but bring a passion to the relationship no sibling can know. The word *mentor* was first found in letters written by fathers for their sons.

The Oxford English Dictionary found the first use of mentor in the year 1750. A father, separated from his home by the challenge of work in a nearby city, was trying to describe what he missed. He used a concept taken from mythology. Mentor was a friend of Odysseus. His name is now synonymous with a faithful and wise advisor. The act of mentoring, the expression felt in a generative relationship, did not appear in our language until the middle of the twentieth century.

Mentoring is as close as many men ever get to fathering. In colonial times, fathers were central to moral and religious education. They also taught their children basics like reading, writing and math. Fathers approved marriages and apportioned family property. They were in control of the family's property because of the universal belief in patriarchy. Exploitation by the patriarch was not one of his most attractive qualities, however, and the concept of patriarchy began to be questioned. The colonial father, however, was "moral overseer, psychologist, and model" and defender of the children against what was believed to be "the emotional, irrational, intellectually inferior and indulgent mother."[37] The obligation and opportunity of fathering was unquestioned in most pre-modern cultures. People didn't need a word like "mentoring" to describe what was a forgone assumption about the father role. This was true of many uncles, craftsmen, ministers and unrelated older villagers as well. Men were the warriors who were to prepare youth for the challenge of being a mature male. They were driven by soulful passion. They were acting as elders.

Elders Not Elderly

There are three ways to be an older person. Most are *elder citizens*. Some are *elderly*. Some tap the archetypal *elder* within and express eldership.

Elder citizens see themselves as being in a state of retirement or wish they were. Although for many retiring is joyful, to retire means to withdraw from business and public life. In fact, "retiring" means retreating, to go backward. The elder who is in the third or fourth quarter of his life retreats in a different way. He retreats into contemplative activities where he discovers the wee small voice. This spiritual message center assures the contemplative person that a movement from self to other is life enhancing, so the retreat into contemplative activity usually leads to an increased need to be with and for other people.

One problem is that in the West, we don't think of people in their fifties, sixties and seventies as being interested in self development and spiritual growth. In China, men and women past the age of fifty are expected to seek self development and make spiritual worship their highest priority. "The older man is the center of contemplation, dwelling…on the action and the power of God."[38] "Aging" in the West includes the assumption that around age fifty we begin an inevitable depletion emotionally, physically, and intellectually.

When you age "successfully,' however, you let loose the "sage in the soul,' "Successful aging" is an activity-oriented approach that increases physical vigor continued intellectual growth. Life-long, yet meaningful work and adequate recreation are also aspects of successful aging. Those who age successfully have a psycho-spiritual model of living that enables them "to complete their life journey, harvest the wisdom of their years and transmit a legacy to future generations.'[39] These are three challenges to the sage within us.

To leave a legacy is to be *saved* to the hard drive of your community's memory. If we buy into the American aging model of *depletion, recreation and retirement,* our long life experience is lost to the generations that follow. Successful aging, then, means more vital involvement for the elder who is *sageing,* while at the same time being a resource to others.[40]

The sage, the elder as mentor, wants to leave a legacy because he has confidence in what life has taught him. If a person follows the *depletion, recreation and retirement* form of late life expression, it suggests that they lack confidence in their wisdom. Wisdom needs to be shared and it drives a person to be accessible to those who need to receive it. The elder has confidence because he has gone within himself and accessed the wee small voice of the soul. Once accomplishing this, the elder hungers to nurture his soul, the soul in others and the soul in the earth that feeds him, supports him and to which he is inexplicably and passionately intertwined.

The elder is more balanced than the elderly. He finds that much of the self-fulfilling aspects of traditional retirement, such as play and travel, enhance a man's sense of balance. He isn't a monk. The elder in America is going to look quite American. He won't be a shaman or a lama. If he feels like a guru to those who benefit from his wisdom, all the better. But, an American elder many dress conservatively or old-fashioned. He may drive too slow, golf a lot, garden and enjoy classes taught at the local senior center. What makes him different is the need those around him feel to be in his presence. The treasure that each elder brings, however, is the potential liberation of the archetypal energies in a man that brings him to be a balanced, mature male. An elder is the spokesman for the community of man. He brings the message that people want a return to the *mature masculine*, which in turn helps maintain the functional family and a lively God-centered spirit.

The elder models the archetypal standards of celebrating life. He finds performing work to be more than a means to earn money—he discovers a joyful expression of self. He rings the bell for the cooperative community living in harmony making decisions using consensus. He respects the Earth and adores the children. The elder speaks for men and women who are equal yet admired for what is deeply feminine and deeply masculine.

❖   ❖   ❖   ❖

Scott, an Elder With Over Fifty Years Life Experience

I am a seeker. I am moved by a spiritual hunger that I sometimes feel in my chest as a pain that scares me.

Scott is one of the male elders I found on my search. He is a contractor who builds roads. He is a father and a full time seeker. He looks for ways to nourish his soul, which in turn affects the way he runs his business and the way he fathers his children. He sometimes appears restless and dissatisfied to his friends and his employees, but they believe he is on a journey that is good for him because he changes and grows. Being with Scott is a calming experience. He has an invigorating energy, yet he is a contemplative man. He is very approachable but has boundaries that keep him safe. I suspect that Scott spends very little time with personal friends because he is so involved in his spiritual journey, his family, his church and his business. He is traditional in his male drive to be responsible, dependable. Nevertheless, his community considers him a young sage, a man with one foot in the universe where all is one.

Scott has been growing psychologically a few years now. He has increasingly found the strength to abstain from behaviors that replaced psychological growth, creativity and good health. All elders have a shadow side, an aspect of self about which they are not proud. But elders, once learning about their shadow, keep an eye on the "beast" so that it does not get out of control. This taming of the beast generates creative energy that can promote growth. At mid-life, Scott increasingly finds himself hungering for more life that is based on a celebration, a harvest of what he has accomplished in the first half of life. As Scott begins to harvest, he finds himself longing for more time to be in nature. He wants what he calls a "conscious, visceral and constant relationship with God." He believes that the closer he gets to this passion, the more he will want to be in the world for people, in service and living a life based on love, not fear.

Chapter II

MATURE MASCULINITY

The joy of being blessed,
Imagined and hoped for.
In my youth needed for growth
At least now,
In my majority, it may
Come from me to thee.

To express mature masculinity, a man must access that part of him that is centered, calming. That place is near the heart. The more time a man spends there, the quicker he matures and grows. A mature man is driven by husbandry and is passionate about advocacy of children, of women and the earth. The man who expresses mature masculinity is stabilizing and courageous. He celebrates his family and enhances its functioning by being present and involved. The mature male, the "deep male," hungers for a passionate and affirming relationship with a partner who embodies his *anima*, the unconscious feminine energy in a man's psyche.

This lucky man has been blessed by a mother's love. He then takes this blessing which has opened his heart, and moves into the realm of father where he learns the skills needed to move aggressively, energetically into the world. Next, this fellow moves away from the father, achieves mastery of what he had been taught and is now capable of mentoring others. When a mature man lives long enough, he reveres life as a cherished gift, hungering to serve others yet understanding his limitations. The mature man accesses deep male energies in the psyche and seeks to explore his life. This man cultivates intimacy and has numerous friends.

The mature man is loyal to something greater than he is: a philosophy, country, leader, family. He arouses excitement in others about his commitment to bettering his community, and he poses a threat to the shadow forces that are devoted to destruction of people and the environment. The mature man is both intuitive and insightful. Children enjoy him because he is playful, compassionate, spiritual and gentle. Women enjoy the mature male because he is confident, nurturing, ordered and empathetic.

The Industrial Era

Those who have been victims of the unloving and dangerous acts of men have met immature men. They are men who live in men's bodies but experience life like a boy. This incongruence is confusing at best, spiritually destructive at worst. As a man ages, he moves through stages of development, but absent that growth, his soul begins to disintegrate as he lives in fear. "The individual unit of evolution is the soul."[41] As a person comes to experience creativity, healing and love, he lives off the energy of the soul. "When the energy of the soul is recognized, acknowledged and valued, it begins to infuse the life of the personality."[42] Soul is the experience of God and it is the place in man that connects him to all men.

Historical events have served to divert our attention from our spirit center, our soul. In the nineteenth century we were diverted by our interest in machines. The conversion was from a rural, extended family to a disembodied family with fathers in the workplace and mothers enclosed in the home alone with the children. Our fascination with machines led to a passion for mass production and profit. Following the potential of the machine led us out of soul.

Men have developed a soulless machine-based image of masculinity. Today men and machines are efficient, productive, autonomous, calculating, in control, tireless, rational and we act like we don't easily break down.[43] The pursuit of profit has become a central theme to "traditional masculinity." Making a living used to be a means to an end.

Even though trading was an important aspect of survival in pre-modern times, selling goods with the goal of making a profit was not the means by which pre-modern cultures solved their economic problems. Economics prior to the eighteenth century was a system based on exchange—goods were simply produced for trade and consumption. About 1700, however, technology got more complicated. Thomas Newcomen patented the steam engine. Then in 1769, James Watt took Newcomen's idea and patented the locomotive engine. Off we went. It became easier to compete and the profit motive for the production of goods was activated.

Up until the eighteenth century, agricultural life had settled into a system of tenant farming under large landowners. Side-by-side with the large estates, common land was used as pasture and for cultivation. With the approach of the Industrial Era in this century, the disruption of the traditional family and small community began. "For sustained contact with the 'world' touched men's innermost experience, indeed their very character. Many of the qualities most readily associated with success in work—ambition, cleverness, aggressive pursuit of the main chance—had no place in domestic life."[44]

Since the beginnings of civilization, manufacturing, construction and industrial activity had been the province of craftsmen who worked out of their homes. Craftsmen formed into guilds and were their own employers, forming a large middle class. Whether they were farmers or craftsmen, the focus of men in this era was on family. Capitalists existed in small numbers. There were no rich manufacturers. The rich were the large landowners, moneylenders and merchants. The coming of manufacturing brought a hunger for wealth because the power of machines made it easier to amass riches. Men's commitment to wealth began to take a toll on body and soul.

Beginning in about 1900 men's life expectancy began to shorten. Until then men and women could expect to live the same amount of time—about forty-nine years. The lifestyle of men and women didn't differ greatly until the men formed into the great masses of workers in the factories. The Great Depression created a loss of soul as well as property and income. Our hunger for wages and profit left us vulnerable to a great emotional depression as our grandfathers lost their jobs in the 1930s. The Great Crash of the stock market was devastating because we were "machine men" finding personal meaning in producing wealth. Pre-modern European farmers worked about 1,600 hours annually, less than half the 3,650 hours worked each year by the average American worker in 1850 and less than the 2,050 hours worked annually by American workers today.[45]

The man, who finds his pathway, grows up and experiences life fully, usually has teachers, mentors or models to admire. Prior to the advent of machinery, master craftsmen provided mentorship to their apprentices. Many young men learned a trade from their fathers because the family worked together on the farm or within the village commons. The eighteenth century man was not very mobile. Life usually began and ended in the same community. On the village common a child could find mentors of many kinds: uncles; neighbors; village merchants; grandparents; and parents. Men and women expected to teach the young. Their close proximity and lack of mobility enhanced their accessibility. Children assumed that older people would be mentors.

Since the nineteenth century restructuring of society, we have redefined the roles of men and women. In industrializing the culture, we not only enclosed men in the factories but left women overwhelmed with parenting and created new mystiques of masculine and feminine. In the sixteenth century and for centuries prior, the village commons were the primary social units of England. All but the royalty, landed gentry, military and church hierarchy lived on the land and tilled it for subsistence. Those who farmed held land as shareholders, making community decisions democratically.

Nuclear families worked side-by-side. Much of the work was assigned by sex. The assumed work roles of men and women varied from country to country, but it was common, for example, that men often planted while women harvested. Children could copy their fathers and mothers because they were both present. Then came the Enclosure Acts in Great Britain that literally "enclosed" the people out of their land. The government supported the goals of the large landowners that were the taxpayers: to fence off land worked by the people and create more space to raise sheep. The economic activities that justified the Enclosure Acts dislodged those who worked the land from the land. The Industrial Revolution completed the process of "enclosing the men" out of the home and into the workplace.

Men drifted toward the new manufacturing regions. There they joined the families of the impoverished and degraded craftsmen in factories. "The immediate effect of the Industrial Revolution upon the countries to which it came, was to cause a vast, distressful shifting and stirring of the mute, uneducated, leaderless, and now more and more property less common population."[46] This "shifting and stirring" began a process that left men's souls undernourished. This social and economic movement of people destroyed communities, created uncounted numbers of economic refugees and disrupted the norms for living of all those it affected.

The shattering of souls began with the forced movement of people from the land and was compounded by the Industrial Revolution two centuries later. When the larger landowners began to build fences to enclose their land and their stock, they also cut off people from their natural interplay with the earth. Being in the land stirs a sense of stewardship, an honoring of the source of life and an understanding of fertility. We celebrate fertility both on the land and in the people. What began in the nineteenth century was an impoverishment—the opposite of fertility. To be impoverished is to have exhausted fertility and the inclination to stewardship. The impoverished desperately approach life with fear. Men act out from a place in their psyche that is survival focused, logical and causes little emotional expression.

Masculine Mystique

Mature masculinity is a heart-centered approach to life that is generative and utterly trustworthy. The immature male is impoverished in his soul and acts from his ego. His heart is less able to influence his being. The impoverishment of men that came out of the time of machines led to a new view of masculinity, a new mystique. The new mystique has resulted in considerable confusion about the difference between mature masculinity and the traditional male role of the twentieth century. For example, emotional people express their feelings. If a man expresses feeling he is still masculine, but society considers him weak. We confuse the emotional, spiritual and intuitive side of a man with what we admire in women. The anima, the unconscious feminine side of a man's nature influences how a man expresses himself. The immature male often tries to repress this internal, opposite archetype because he approaches others more from ego than from soul.

Mature masculinity is manifested in men who access, in a balanced way, the individual and collective energies of maleness in the psyche—the conscious and unconscious aspects of the human personality. Mature masculinity is the most complete expression of a man's self. When a movement away from heart has impoverished the soul, the center of the psyche is too deep to access. Men moved away from their heart center when they left the land and the family. Their sense of mental, physical, psychological and spiritual balance was diminished in this move.

In the 1960s, women challenged the then "feminine mystique." Women were in large part expressing dissatisfaction with the behavior of the immature male. Expressing the immature masculine, men have been controlling and threatening. They have deprived women of their effectiveness. Women suffered the embarrassment and disrespect of the patriarchal husband and father. Women have been ridiculed, laughed at and held down by the man who is still a boy inside.

No longer were women willing to submit to the domestic plan that had evolved from the Industrial Era. In particular they resented patriarchy. The feminist wanted men who considered women their equal, who spent time with the family. The problem was that immature men, who were out of touch with the deep male archetypes within their psyche, didn't know how to grow up.

The masculine mystique has not been confronted with nearly the same force as has the feminine mystique. Not only have we let immature maleness divert us from full expression, but the feminists born of the women's movement have also been very intimidating. Their aggressive expression of rights has been seen by the boys-in-men's-bodies as emasculation. A mature man understands and respects assertiveness. A boy often interprets it as aggression. So while there has been an assault on the feminine mystique, Western people's acceptance of the masculine mystique has fostered a remarkable silence concerning the ongoing destruction of mature maleness.

The hatred that women feel coming from immature men has today been matched by a general misandry: a hate of men. This hate combined with the grief many men experience has led to a greater emotional and physical vulnerability. At the turn of the twentieth century, life expectancy was equal for men and women. Today, however, "If power means having control over your own life, then perhaps there is no better ranking of the impact of sex roles…on power over our lives than life expectancy. Here is the ranking:

-Females (white)   79 years

-Females (black)   74 years

-Males (white)   72 years

-Males (black)   65 years[47]

Many factors influence life expectancy, and misandry alone can't be blamed. The issue is men's sense of personal power. We lost touch with how a person plays an effective part in community by isolating ourselves in the workplace. We aggravated the problem of patriarchy by being away from home so much. In the twentieth century we surveyed this problem. The survey has left many men feeling guilty and unsure of how to behave. This reduces a man's sense of potency.

The Rest of the Statistics

A measure of powerlessness is the rate of suicide. As Warren Farrell *in The Myth of Male Power* asserts, until boys are nine years old, suicide rates are as low as girl's. From ten to fourteen years the boys' rate is twice as high. From fifteen to nineteen years, four times as high and from twenty to twenty-four, six times that of girls. The suicide rate for men over eighty-five is 1,350 percent higher than for women of the same age group.[48]

The hate of men has led into false assumptions about men's power. As a minority of men perpetuates domestic violence, the overall impact of violent crime is *on* men, not only *by* men. Men are three times more likely than women to be victims of murder and twice as likely to be victims of other violent crimes. Over the past thirty years the cancer death rate for men has increased 21 percent while the rate for women has remained the same. Men represent 55 percent of the work force but 93 percent of all job-related deaths.[49] Increasingly powerless men are very vulnerable.

Power is also defined in terms of money and property. The masculine mystique includes the belief that men have more of both. The U.S. Dept. of Commerce, Bureau of the Census tells us that women's financial worth is considerably higher than men's. Take the wealthiest Americans: among the top 1.6 percent of the U.S. population, women's net worth is greater than men's. With men living shorter lives, women are left with the wealth. Women also have greater spending power and lower spending obligations.[50] This is not to say women are the problem. Women are filling gaps left by men who leave the home, rush head-long after power for power's sake and die too young. The men end up with enough stress to detach emotionally and not enough health to avoid deadly illness.

The U.S. Department of Labor reports that about one million men in their prime working years have stopped looking for jobs. Not only are many just sitting home, but in 1995 dollars, the weekly wage of those males working has dropped from $611 in 1979 to $538 in 1995. Women, meanwhile, have been increasing their activity in the workforce and their average wage has been increasing. Women have been less impacted by the loss of manufacturing jobs to low-wage countries and white-collar jobs being replaced by computers. Women are even less affected by affirmative action policy.

Being male can be discouraging. Andrew Kimbrell, in his important book, *The Masculine Mystique,* found that boys are twice as likely as girls to suffer from autism and eight times more likely to be treated for hyperactivity. He says two-thirds of special education is devoted to boys and that over 60 percent of high school dropouts are male. More women graduate from college than do men. Kimbrell estimated that 270,000 of our veterans are homeless and that 70 percent of the homeless are single men. Men's economic and political power is at risk in light of these facts.

Men are torn between their commitment to provide and their desire to be emotionally attached to those they love. Nearly 80 percent of married men with preschool children are employed full-time. Half of all marriages disintegrate with men receiving custody of the children in less than 20 percent of contested divorce actions. And then immature masculinity leads to absent non-custodial fathers. One out of five divorced fathers see their children as little as once a year. One out of every two sees his children only "several times a year."[51] Men have lost hope about their role in parenting. Finding time in their work-a-day lives to be with their families is hard.

Boys in Men's Bodies

The immature male of today demonstrates how it looks to be fragmented with "various parts of his personality…split off from each other and leading…independent and often chaotic lives…. He remains a boy, not because he wants to, but because no one has shown him the way to transform his boy energy into man energies." In this quote from Robert Moore's book, *King, Warrior, Magician, Lover,* the author expresses a view of immaturity that suggests men are victims of our transition into modernity.

The man who abuses his children, the politician who takes advantage of his constituency, the minister who hates homosexuals, the gang-banger who inflicts pain, the absent father and the tyrant boss all have one thing in common. They are all boys-in-men's-bodies. The community mistakes these oversized boys for mature men. Moore suggests that these men model "boy psychology" when what the world needs is men who have been initiated into "man psychology." Boy psychology is an expression of immature masculinity, the stunted masculine stuck at early stages of development.

Traditional masculinity is what we have come to believe is standard male stuff. It includes "the requirement to avoid all things feminine; the injunction to restrict ones emotional life; the emphasis on toughness and aggression; the injunction to be self- reliant; the emphasis on achieving status above all else; nonrelational, objectifying attitudes toward sexuality."[52] These traits of what has come to be known as traditional masculinity are nearly all expressions of boy psychology. In the balanced male we find a nurturing, emotional and generous being. These "feminine" traits are an expression of both men and women who are soulful, fearless and honest. Toughness and aggression work for those who love and respect the rights of others while also believing in their own rights. What the immature male has done is express toughness for its own sake thinking this alone will gain him status.

Achieving status becomes necessary for the man or woman who is not secure celebrating who they truly are. Status is usually achieved through accomplishment, wealth or celebrity. Self-reliance is a more balanced trait. Mature men express it. Pretending to be stronger by acting without help, without the support of others, is risky. It might be good recreation on occasion but as a regular practice, for its own sake, it is immature and unbalanced.

Philosopher Gabriel Marcel said that those who reduce a mystery to a problem are guilty of intellectual perversion.[53] Immature men often miss the fact that sexual encounter is an experience in mystery and intimacy. Objectifying sex means to approach another person in a disembodied way. The opposite of objectifying sex is making it an intimate and innermost experience of joining in spirit with a woman. This is difficult for the sensation driven boy-in-a-man's-body to grasp.

Too Many Bullies and Cowards

Unlike the questions that exist today about what a man is or should be, in the 1950's when I was becoming a man, most of us took gender roles for granted. When I was in high school, I represented one of the two kinds of boys that existed in too great a number: bullies and cowards. Both types experience underdeveloped masculine energy. The second type was represented well by Peyton.

The fear I felt when Peyton tripped or humiliated me in some way was rooted in underdeveloped warrior energy. I didn't get angry, I got scared. Peyton could smell my fear. He tripped me in the hallway at Anchorage High because he knew instinctively that I was afraid of him. He was angry at the world and I was intimidated by it. The boy under the influence of this aggressive energy doesn't have his feelings and mind under control. Control and balance come with maturity.

Peyton and I were operating out of the shadow side of our psyche. The shadow usually contains inferior qualities that are balanced by a good self-esteem. If we don't remain conscious of the power of our dark side, it can push us in a dark direction. The boys-in-men's-bodies are out of balance and they respond too willingly to shadow energy. The insensitive, fearful energy in the psyche of these boys is running their life. "The Shadow Warrior carries into adulthood that adolescent insecurity, violent emotionalism and desperation of the [archetypal] Hero."[54] The archetypal energy of the underdeveloped Warrior interferes with intimacy.

Peyton the bully and I were raised in the 40s and 50s by parents raised in the Depression. Our grandparents, who also lived in a time of transition, raised our parents. Theirs was a transition from rural to industrial America. Our grandparents and our parents were focused on earning a living and having wealth. Their ancestors had been in the land and were driven by a desire to survive. Peyton's father and mine were victims of the separation of men from the land and the subsequent change into the lifestyle of a wage earner. Over the last couple of centuries, wage earners have been preoccupied with earning an income. Before the enclosure of men into the workplace, men worked to survive and to express creativity. In striving for the fruits of their labor, Industrial Era workers lost touch with the harvest of self and the spirit. Because our fathers had lost touch with their center, their soul, they failed to model mature masculinity. Modern men's access to mature masculine energy in the psyche had been reduced by this travesty.

Peyton was angry because he was emotionally impoverished. I was vulnerable and frightened for the same reason. We were boys who lacked the mentoring needed to show us how to access mature masculine energy. We learned from our mothers what was preferred male behavior. Our mothers' influence was greater than our fathers' because the men were emotionally detached from their soul, physically removed from their home and their children. Following our mothers, then, led us to "put down our swords." We forgot at that point that although it can be dangerous, use of the sword by a mature man is motivating, invigorating and positive.

Boys at Work

As an employee assistance professional, I have been witnessing traditional masculinity in the workplace. An employee assistance counselor assists people at work to prevent and treat mental health and other personal problems. In this work, I see how immature masculinity leads to an imbalance of a man's mental condition. Men at work in business and industry have less time with their families and increased pressure to compete, which leads to a hunger for status and power, a guarded interpersonal style, a fear of termination and a belief that wealth and status measure them. I am as good an example as any.

I am the chief executive officer of my consulting firm. Carrying this title satisfies my need for power. I am not simply the elder of our company, or the owner, or the most respected, but the CEO! The challenge for me is to separate the power I have from the *power-over* I have. On the occasions that I am aware of my personal power, I experience it as influence, but it is also generative. I feel like a steward. If I wield my status, my power, I lose a connection to the people who work for me. I lose their cooperation. The more cooperation I facilitate, the more we all accomplish.

The spiritless bullies like Peyton want power-over. When I operate from my fear, my "inner coward," I want power-over also. Men who are still like boys are often in charge at work, but they are paradoxically powerless. Their influence ends when the employee goes home. While the employee is at work, he is putting up with the immature boss, not supporting him or working toward consensus. Men like me are products of an industrial world. Those inclined to be involved in activity that nourishes the soul are constantly dancing with maintaining the balance between power and power-over, competition and cooperation, and fear and love.

There are too many examples of traditional masculinity in the workplace. The workplace expression of immature masculinity has led to the need for nondiscrimination policies in most companies. We need rules nowadays to discourage sexual harassment at work. Policies are written on how to cope with violence at work, the perpetrators of which are men.

Pre-modern men worked so that they could have food and shelter. Their work was a natural response to basic needs like survival and hunger. Then, one day, it was discovered that "things," once created by work, could be traded. Trading allowed for needs to be met without working. So the drive to satisfy basic needs led to work which, in turn, led to the creation of goods that could be either used or traded. Artists showed us that some things could be created for their own sake. This included gems, paintings and statuary. We also created things for their own sake that could be counted and accumulated. We discovered that we could accumulate more than other people could and that the other people envied us. The accumulation of lots of envied things led to the admiration of wealth. Somewhere between creating things for their own sake and creating wealth, some of us lost touch with our soul. Accumulating is fine until it becomes more important than the reason a man exists on Earth.

The Machines

In the Industrial Era, man figured out how to create things faster by using machines. Once we created machines, we recreated our image of ourselves. "As we cast, soldered, burned and molded the ore and fossil fuels of the Earth to fashion the great engines of the industrial age, these machines just as surely recast and remolded modern consciousness."[55] Modern man's work and play are concerned with integrating machines into our life. Machines like televisions, computers and telephones are required for any who can afford them. We learn with machines. We communicate with machines. We travel with machines.

The image of maleness that has led to our impoverishment is like the image we have of machines. Depending on machines can turn us into machine men. To the machine man even sexuality becomes a technical skill. The male lover becomes a "love machine." The machine man "becomes part of the total machinery that he controls and is simultaneously controlled by. He has no plan or goal in life, except doing what the logic of technique determines him to do…Robots are among the greatest achievement of his technical mind, and some specialists assure us that the robot will hardly be distinguished from living men."[56]

Machine men are to be efficient problem solvers, who bring home the bacon, which is proof of our productive nature. We are in control and rational and, most of all, efficient. The most longed for trait of a good machine is efficiency. To compete successfully, we need to work long hours with little attention given to our health. While we are not yet cyborgs, we have "a homogenized masculine image modeled on the machine. This dehumanized 'machine man' is the sine qua non of the masculine mystique. He represents the triumph of the mechanized over the organic, of technology over men."[57] The most profound impact the machine man model has on us is to starve the soul. Machine men are more like replaceable parts than passionate beings. They are expendable.

"Men did a better job creating better homes and gardens for their wives than they did creating safer coal mines and construction sites for themselves. Few cared that only men died by thousands clearing paths through mountains to build roads for cars and trucks for trains that allowed the rest of civilization to be served in a dining car."[58] If a man succeeds at this work he is credited with being a "male machine." Only the male machines are sent to war. Female machines can be in the military but they aren't allowed to die on purpose. Male machines, like real machines, are dispensable. In the Battle of Somme, 1916, a single battle of WWI, British casualties were 420,000, French were 195,000 and German, 650,000! They were all men.[59]

Competition

Another commitment men made as they became producers in the industrialized and mechanized world of work was to compete—to compete for jobs, the best pay, the most success and the highest level of job assignment. The force that both binds and divides men is competition. Particularly when men meet in a new place, they begin to measure one another for strength and position. This nearly uncontrollable process goes on in corporate conference rooms as well as at "new age" gatherings.

In the mind of the competitor, taking a sick day away from the "grind" means:

- His territory is threatened and someone might usurp his position
- Someone might discover he really isn't needed or might try to replace him
- Each day in bed is money lost
- He's not a capable warrior and doesn't hold up under pressure [60]

In competition, the questions are: Who's winning?, How much was his bonus?, Who wants to go first? Most men remember the humiliation they felt when they weren't successful on the playground or athletic field. We jokingly report, "Yeah, I never got picked." Only a small number of people win. To the traditional twenty-first century man, needing to express aggression and toughness, he feels he must compete. Competition, of course, is not an experience in intimacy. The man who restricts his emotional life and needs to achieve status is drawn to compete if only in a minor way. "We are told that real men don't ask for help but only the 'opportunity' to compete…. As competition becomes the male's main avenue of self-validation, fear of losing in competition remains the single greatest anxiety for many men."[61]

Even with similar abilities, people oriented toward mastery and hard work typically achieve more if they avoid competing. Competition in business and sports can lead to better services, new products and higher scores. There are, however, psychological hazards to competition. Competition is the opposite of cooperation. "Healthy competition" can be a contradiction. Competition often leads to insecurity, anxiety, jealousy and hostility.

Men Do, Women Be

Since the 1950s, many sociologists and psychologists have agreed with the *instrumental/expressive* divide between men and women. This is a product of the belief that men are primarily oriented toward activity, achievement and power. Women are believed to be oriented toward nurturance and relationship.[62] The traditional male, he, who reinforces the masculine mystique, risks getting lost while seeking achievement and power. He gets lost in "doing"! Warren Farrell said, "women are human beings. Men are humans doing." The experience we have with mature masculinity, on the other hand, is that activity, achievement and power are integrated with a hunger for cooperation, mastery and intimacy. Men are oriented differently than women, hence, the wonderful energy that is created when men and women interplay.

It is likely that men and women are literally hard-wired in different ways.[63] Perhaps men's pre-modern hunter role has contributed to their inclination to be aggressive. Men are better at reading maps, finding their way geographically and targeting with a weapon. Women's childbearing and food gathering roles have created nurturing skills. They are more capable in interpersonal communications. They are more sensitive to touch and have greater dexterity.

Gender differences can be culturally influenced, however. Men and women can be taught to behave differently than evolution has delivered them. One of the most infamous examples is the impact of replacing the farm with the factory. The workplace valued instrumental qualities that men have such as their better-developed spatial view. Home life requires expressive qualities such as those of the childcare specialists—women. The Industrial Revolution was so powerful culturally that it restyled the meaning of manhood. This era enforced the position of women locked into the home. It gradually tore the fabric of masculine expression and left behind the distortion that today we call traditional masculinity.

Fatherlessness

Historically men have showed an inclination to four functions in most societies: *protector, provider, teacher and authority figure.* Women have shifted emphasis away from being the primary caretaker of children and the primary force in homemaking. They are increasingly interested in playing the four male roles. Men are less needed, therefore, in their historical roles and are being asked to participate more in childbearing and other "domestic pursuits." Although a man may willingly assume the title of biological father, the activity level varies.

because men's productive and parental strategies are variable, culture is central to enforcing high paternal investment. In every society the main cultural institution designed for this purpose is marriage. Father involvement with children is closely linked to the quality of the relationship between husband and wife.[64]

In this quote from David Popenoe's landmark book, *Life Without Father,* the author asserts that men's inclination to fathering is reinforced by cultural ties with marriage, being the strongest cultural linkage of all. But the divorce rate is still on the rise with custody usually going to the mother. Biological fathers are considered more and more dispensable. Nearly 30 percent of all births in the USA are to unmarried women. Boys are increasingly growing up without a male model they can trust. Femininity in daughters is related directly to the father's masculinity model. A father's approval of the mother as a model of femininity and the father's encouragement of his daughter's participation in feminine activities facilitate the development of healthy feminine expression. An absent father, therefore, affects the development of both healthy femininity in girls and masculinity in boys. More than ever before, fathers are living apart from their biological children. The primary causes:

- High divorce rate
- Custody after divorce is usually given to mothers (86 percent of single parent families are run by women.)
- Out-of-wedlock births
- Emotional detachment brought on by the masculine mystique
- An increase in non-marital co-habitation and resultant instability (50 percent of cohabitiating couples have children.) [65]

Most of these causes result from voluntary choices made by fathers.

Just prior to the 1960s revolutions in women's rights and sexual expression, more children were living with both of their natural parents than at any other time in world history.[66] The rate, however, has been dropping ever since. It has been estimated that only one out of two children born in 1980 will be living with their biological parents by age seventeen. Half of all adult Americans under the age of forty have cohabited. About 3.5 million cohabiting couples are living in the United States. This is up from 2 million only ten years ago.[67]

Since 1960 there has been a significant decline in men's interest in having children. By 1992 only about 5 percent of all female-headed households with children had experienced the death of the husband. So where was he? About 37 percent of these households had experienced divorce. In roughly a third of these homes, the parents had never married. For the first time in our nation's history, men are voluntarily abdicating fatherhood in large numbers.[68]

The status of marriage has shifted. A standard American sentiment: It is best for the children to get a divorce if the parents can't get along. Popenoe suggests that marriage has become one of the least binding of legal contracts. The modern marriage is a kind of temporary business partnership with an illusory contract in which neither party involved will be held liable for breaking any promises that are made.[69]

Are the children better off?

Let's start building the answer to this question with the issue of presence. Can a father realistically maintain a significant level of intimacy if he is not in custody of the children and in their presence? Among children from marriages that were disrupted ten or more years before, only one in ten had weekly contact with their fathers. Almost two-thirds had no contact during the past year. Nearly 30 percent of remarried fathers never see their children.[70]

The separation between child and non-custodial parent doesn't simply come after divorce, however. About 30 percent of American births occur outside of marriage. This is up considerably since 1960 when it was around 5 percent. Most of these out-of-wedlock births are to unattached women, not cohabiting women.[71] By 1990, households with nuclear families, that is families with two married adults with children, were down to 26 percent of total from 44 percent before the revolutions of the 1960s.

The impact of these changes in family structure on children is even greater because of our drive toward self-fulfillment. This turn inward in search of self has been prominent in the present generation of adults. There has been a shift toward individualism while at the same time movement away from social concern. Examples of this are found in the drop in volunteerism and declining church attendance. Marriage and family have always been our pivotal social institutions. Some suggest that when we focus our energy on self-development, the family suffers.

The shift toward individualism has also been accentuated by our hunger for material affluence. Our wealth provides the wherewithal to pursue an individualistic and private lifestyle separate from the society around us. Americans have a number of culturally designed behaviors and beliefs that can lead to the harm of children and cause fatherhood to be less needed. These include:

- Making marriage into a dispensable institution
- Sexualizing society
- Pretending the only adult role of importance is the work role
- Playing down that marriage and children are a major part of a man' life
- Having an economic system that doesn't recognize worker's family responsibility
- Developing a culture that stresses individualism over social responsibility
- De-emphasizing the importance of children to the continuation of society
- Overlooking the fathering role when teaching male gender expression
- Encouraging the problematic idea that fathers should become more like mothers

These beliefs and behaviors lead to less father presence. It does not appear that father influence can be as real where the father is less visible or less confidant of his value. The extreme of the less visible father is fatherlessness. Men usually need to be in a committed relationship to develop a passion for fathering. And once he becomes a parent, his presence is essential to the healthy development of both femininity in their daughters and masculinity in their sons. However, increasing numbers of fathers are living apart from their children. The institution of marriage is declining in its appeal in the West and this has led to the disappearance of a present and visible father.

Juvenile crime has increased over three times since 1965.[72] Since 1976 reports of child neglect and abuse have risen by over 250 percent.[73] Eating disorders and depression among adolescent girls have skyrocketed. Alcohol and other drug abuse remains high. SAT scores have declined.

The most mature role a man will ever play is father. Married fatherhood is a man's most important pathway to happiness. There is a civilizing effect on men in simply being in the company of a wife and a child. "No longer a social accident, many fathers are active partners in parenthood."[74] They are essential to the fullest, most functional life of the child. Fathers are probably more important today than ever before. The whole village no longer raises children. Mothers are increasingly absent as they leave home for work.

Historical Fatherhood

In the pre-industrial world a clear standard of manhood prevailed. To be fulfilled as a man, an adult male, if firstborn, took ownership of land from his father, successfully headed a household and carefully guided the destiny of his children.[75] However, the enclosure of men out of the home and a new admiration of children gradually placed women in a preeminent household role. The rejection of the Calvinist notion of innate child depravity in the eighteenth century made reasonable the shifting of children's care to the maternal, less instrumental parent. The man's role as teacher and carrier of cultural history gave way to public mandatory education. The new respect for children caused the community to create social welfare and educational systems that began to replace traditional family function.

Despite its patriarchal qualities, what we now call the "nuclear family" represented for women a significant advance over their situation in the pre-modern family. Throughout the nineteenth century more women married, bore children who survived and had husbands who lived jointly with them. The nineteenth century Victorian family became more of a partnership than a hierarchy. Male authority became symbolic as respect for women grew and mothers began to develop domestic influence.[76]

The shift in the definition of masculinity away from protector and provider toward self-aggrandizing individualist resulted in the diminished influence of fathers. Male interest in a new expression drew men together in groups. Fraternal orders began to grow in the late nineteenth century. The humor of men in these clubs grew disparaging of marriage, the dominance of women and family responsibilities. In reaction, women and children began to buy the masculine mystique. Males, including fathers, were viewed as inherently suspect. Masculinity was felt to pose the threat of tempting fathers away from the home. "From being considered a central, natural and unproblematic aspect of being a man, as it had been with the Puritans, fatherhood became something which needed to be promoted by the culture."[77] Today, numerous social scientists suggest that the father is no longer even necessary to the economic survival of the family.

The "work world" that has had such a devastating impact on men's inclination to fathering has become suspect. A man's morality is in question when he spends excessive time at work. The early factories were disordered and unstable. Some felt they destabilized male workers and made them vulnerable to vices and other less than civilized behaviors. Personal integrity was largely discounted in the workplace of the nineteenth century. "The men who lived and worked in this environment were necessarily imperiled and maleness itself seemed to carry a certain odor of contamination."[78] The dark side of the work world looms large for families who want more of Dad's time at home.

For the first time in history a war brought the drafting of fathers. The departure of fathers in World War II strengthened their importance while at the same time adding to the causes of fatherlessness. However, the return of the father/war hero was celebrated by the nuclear family in a way not experienced in a long time. For several years after the war and into the 1950s, the value of fathers was remembered thusly:

- Fathers are protectors if for no other reason than their greater size.
- Fathers provide, albeit not all by themselves.
- Fathers are the primary male role models.
- Fathers provide a second adult for raising children, to teach coping skills in a male-dominated work world.
- Fathers emphasize play more than mothers.
- Fathers model competitive skills, showing initiative, risk taking and assertiveness.
- Father presence in the home helps reduce teen delinquency and the incidence of teen pregnancy.
- Fathers are often the disciplinarian of last resort.
- Fathers are the parent that fosters good quantitative and verbal skills and improved problem solving ability.
- Fathers foster empathetic concern and self-control.
- Fathers often foster extroversion and independence.
- Fathers' presence allows mothers more opportunity for a more involved and multi-faceted life experience.

Where Does Father Fit Today?

David Popenoe reports on a fascinating study done with adolescent girls in the early 1970s. The researchers separated the girls into three groups: 1) Those from an intact, father-present family 2) Those who had lost their fathers through divorce 3) Those who had lost their fathers through death. A male interviewer offered the subjects any of three places to sit near his desk. The girls in group one generally chose to sit in a chair that was at a medium-distance from the interviewer, while the second group of girls sat closer and acted more seductively. The girls in group three sat far away and tended to be rigid and quiet. The girls whose father raised them related to the male interviewer naturally and with ease.[79]

More than one critic of men as parents has quoted anthropologist Margaret Mead's statement that fathers were a biological necessity but a social accident. Later in her career, however, she wrote, "There are things I've written about [fathers] I've regretted, especially that there is no biological basis in them for paternal behavior. I've seen how wrong I was—if you leave a father alone with his baby...the two of them automatically become exceedingly attached to one another."[80]

Modern anthropologists agree with Mead but increasingly report that the roles toward which men are biologically most inclined are the very ones for which they are needed less and less. Many believe that men's commitment to child-rearing is related directly to the commitment they feel from their female partner. The sexual revolution, the increase in cohabiting and out-of-wedlock births all ameliorate against marital commitment. At the very time in history when fathers are badly needed, the cultural ties necessary to hold them have withered.

Today we have families that feel isolated from relatives and their surrounding community. The burden of parenting has increasingly fallen to the nuclear family. At the same time, the father is disappearing. Until the cultural revolutions of the 1960s and 1970s, fathers were considered by most social scientists as core to the "most important moral and legal rule concerning the physiological site of kinship: no child should be brought into the world without a man assuming the role of father, the male link between the child and the rest of the community."[81]

There is hope in the behavior of what some call the "New Father." As preparing for childbirth became a couple-focused process in the 1970s, we began to see more clearly how men were participating actively in preparing for the most important role of their life. In 1980 I began facilitating expectant father classes in Portland, Oregon. These were consciousness-raising groups for men. It was extraordinary for men to sit in a group and discuss preparing for fatherhood. Some were confident, others were nervous and frightened. But they all wanted to learn more about pregnancy, their role in it and wanted to hear what other men thought of it. It is these men who have fought their way into delivery rooms and changed obstetrics to what it is today—men are an active and essential part of the birthing experience.

As an advocate for fathers, I applaud much of the vision of the New Father. Who doesn't admire hands-on, involved fatherhood? However, the most admirable theme of the New Father model—the imploring of men to act tenderly toward their children—is not new at all. Eighteenth century philosopher Jean-Jacques Rousseau said, in speaking about the family, that "The habit of living together gave rise to the sweetest sentiments known to men: conjugal love and paternal love." The New Father reminds us that some men are following their intuition to be complete human beings. Men prompted by soul and their intuition preserve themselves, derive pleasure from their connection to men and women, and openly and spontaneously share their feelings and dreams. The New Father personalizes rather than objectifies relationships. Parenting means responding to the cues of his children and his lover so all may thrive on his willingness to fully express his humanness.

Fatherlessness is possibly the most damaging of the changes brought about by embracing the masculine mystique. We have grown up with the expectation that our fathers will either leave the family or, if present, will be detached from us emotionally or physically because of their need to be at work. We have forgotten what "traditional men and fathers" means. What we have come to believe it means is what the masculine mystique causes it to look like. The seat of archetypal, inborn patterns of male experience is the soul. Buried, within reach, in our psyche are models of masculinity that prevailed for thousands of years. It was only a couple of hundred years ago that we lost touch with our male spirit.

❖   ❖   ❖   ❖

John, an elder with over sixty years life experience

Today, I know what the vows were about. Today I think about my wife during the day and can't wait to get home to see her again. Sometimes I call her in the morning to wake her up. When I'm home, I bring her coffee to her every morning.

I plan to do this the rest of my life.

My friend John can often call upon his elder energy. He is passionate about his wife but admits that when first married, he didn't understand what a committed union meant. He said that back then he gave little thought to what he could do for her but was concerned mostly with his comfort and pleasure. His marriage has lasted thirty-six years, he said, because his wife took their marriage vows seriously. At mid-life, however, John says he has figured out how he wants to be with his wife. "Give much more than you take" is the rule now, he says. Empty the garbage, be where you say you will be. Give her back rubs. Write her love notes and leave them on the bathroom mirror. Write down and remember birthdays and anniversaries for her, the children and the grandchildren.

"After thirty-six years she is still beautiful but we both have worn out a bit," John told me. "The skin that was so smooth to the touch is wrinkled. Her bright eyes are a little red at times and there are deep lines around them. I resist drifting and being with younger women by seeing her eyes with the stains of the many tears she shed over me when I was more selfish. I keep focused on my commitment to her by remembering how she held me and the children with arms that, today, are very tired at times. Today, her arms hold me and I hold her, just because it feels so good to be so close."

Chapter III

THE ELDER IN HISTORY

Three generations away from the farm
Kissed no more by family,
Arm in arm
Mentor me in sympathy
For I long to become
For my child, for the Earth: elder.

M en and women reach mid-life today feeling that things have changed. Many look about and see increasingly healthy fifty and sixty year olds who will probably live until they are ninety or 100 years old—possibly more. An increasing number of people are entering the second half of life not at all clear about how they want to spend their expanded time. At age eighty, my father is vital despite some physical depletion. He is of the generation that arrived at mid-life with a sense that being a "senior citizen" was *not* the first stage of dying. His generation was the first to experience a new longevity. His father, on the other hand, had just a few years past the date he quit work to settle his affairs before death.

My grandfather did not enter the "new life that begins at age sixty" like my father and I. This New Life had not been experienced by people until the last couple of generations. It is a generation—long stage of development. Born during the Industrial Revolution, he worked as a shipfitter in a manufacturing plant making warships. Long hours compromised his health. He not only worked until age sixty-five, but for forty years worked a much longer work day than his predecessors who had been subsistence farmers. He was very tired when he reached age sixty. He lacked energy for and had little interest in improving the Earth, fighting poverty, being a mentor to his grandchildren or volunteering for community improvement projects. I have no memory of time spent walking with him, hearing his wisdom or even standing close by him. He offered a warm smile but was always distant. It felt to me that he was empty and that he didn't have the ability to connect with children.

The elders of history prior to the industrial era didn't usually disengage from life in the way my grandfather did. On the contrary, they often became the interpreters of the moral sector of society. The disengagement characterized by my grandfather was evidence of the impoverishment of men enclosed into the factories. By contrast, this generation—long New Life after sixty we are living in the twenty-first century, has the potential to be "the first step in a total process of transition and reengagement, a process that reached its natural terminus in [an older] society but that is interrupted or aborted" in a society like we see in the West of the twenty-first century.[82]

This "new class of the old" are freer than all other developmental groups before them "to write in their own unique and original part, to lay out the new pattern of creative liberty…They will see that as they are the latest achievement of the life process…they may…cooperate with it by specific conscious development."[83] My grandfather's generation disengaged, pulled away and hid out. They lacked pride in their wisdom. Before today's new class of the old can live their long life in celebration, they must become like the elders of old.

Rabbi Zalman Schachter, author of *From Age-ing to Sage-ing,* writes that our western culture does not have a *bar mitzvah* at retirement. There is no ritual to initiate a man into old age because life after fifty has not been seen as a stage of development. There are few good models so far. There needs to be a new emphasis, a new direction for older people. If, however, we lack role models for eldership, how does this growing crowd of elder citizens become empowered? If people want to learn how to behave elder-like in the second half of life, they need to find out what is needed from them. What is it that people and the Earth need from elders?

And further, they need to ask themselves, "What has my life experience given me from which I can now synthesize wisdom?" To address these questions, let's look back at what we know about elders in history.

Ancient Elders

One of the oldest sources is a book of allegory that most Christians and numerous others consider compelling as an historical work. The Bible, in its many versions contains references to a class of elder people who served as overseers, watchers or guardians. In the earliest days of the New Testament, beginning about 50 AD, each Christian community was influenced by a body of elders who were appointed by the apostles or their representatives. These men were celebrated because they could capture the interest, devotion and confidence of others. Even the tribal chieftains were inclined to bend their will to that of the councils of elders. This community structure copied one that dates back to the time of Moses.

The Old Testament Mediterranean world was patriarchal, but communities in Moses' time were defined more by territorial ties than by family lines. In this tribe-oriented society, the patriarch had less authority than he had exercised in prior nomadic times. There was no king in Israel at that time. Communal decisions were the province of the elders, the heads of the families acting as a body. Moses had dictated further that to qualify as an elder one must be wise, shrewd and tested. The elders were the older men of the tribe. The words *eldest* and *elderly*, which come from the word *elder*, refer to older people, suggesting that the elders of the Bible were among the oldest. Given that the life span in 1000 BC was half that of modern men, biblical elders attained the status of wise men while still raising young children, still being new at their vocations and still in the early stages of accumulating wisdom. Nevertheless, it was assumed that the last stage of life for many was a time of making decisions relevant to the welfare of the community.

The role of the elder included hosting religious ceremonies, acting as arbitrators and answering questions about the proper way to raise children. "If a man has a stubborn and rebellious son who will not listen to the voice of his father or the voice of his mother...[they] shall take hold of him and bring him out to the elders of the town..." (Deut.

21:18-20). Moses' father-in-law advised him to draw upon the strength and sensitivity of these wisemen "so making things easier for you and sharing the burden with you." (Exodus 18:22). Moses sought out the most "trustworthy and incorruptible for the job." Age and prosperity were only two factors leading to the selection of an elder.

In the New Testament, the Apostle Paul wrote in the book of Timothy that to be an elder is noble work and required a man of impeccable character. Character was judged in part by the elder's commitment to having one wife and well-behaved children. Those selected were temperate, courteous, hospitable and even-tempered. Elders were to be "hospitable and a friend of all that is good, sensible, moral, devout and self-controlled..." (Titus 1:5-9). To become an elder, a man did not apparently need to be of high social class. The villages of the eastern Mediterranean in the first centuries after the birth of Christ were not highly stratified. Despite the fact that some older Israelites or Egyptians held property, stock and other measures of wealth, this was not a determinant for selection as an elder. The elder "must not be a lover of money." (I Timothy.3:4). "The love of money is the root of all evils..." (I Timothy 6:10). The most honored function of the elder was to teach.

The elder who was an effective teacher was considered beyond reproach. For example, any accusation of wrongdoing by an elder had to be supported by at least two witnesses. The teaching done by an elder was to be spiritual in nature; their job was to interpret for the student the highest and purest moral nature of man. The elder of biblical times was concerned with the sacred and was "God's representative." So our earliest model for the role of sage is a holy man. The world's spiritual traditions all offer models of elders. In Zen Buddhism you find the *roshi*. Among the Russian Orthodox there was the *staretz,* who literally was a sage who functioned as a spiritual director. There was the *sheikh* in Islam and the *lama* in Tibetan Buddhism. In Judaism one finds the *rebbe*, who was held in higher regard than even the rabbi.

Primitive Eldership

In earliest times the most honored elders were women. Until a few thousand years ago, when it was discovered that men participated in the conception of a child, clans of people determined their lineage through the mothers. The earliest religious symbols and carvings were of goddess-like creatures. Men utilized their extraordinary strength to protect the women who provided the men with sex and shared in the tasks of survival. As time moved on and clans of people stopped wandering and began to collect goods, the job of protector became more important. The role expanded to include protecting the family's "things" as well as the people in the family. The more things, the more important the protector became. Thus enters the *pater familias*, the male patriarch. His power was to remain nearly unquestioned as head of the family until the eighteenth century. Some of these patriarchs were elders. Most were simply "in power" by reason of their sex and paternity.

In Roman times, changes in family relationships emerged because of the wars that characterized the Empire's history. The spoils of war had always been treated as the property of the soldier's family and controlled by the patriarch of the family. With so many conquests, however, the soldier, with the increasing support of the government, was able to keep his booty and build up his own estate separate from that of his father's family. Additionally, women's liberation glimmered a bit as absent patriarchs were forced to share with the women male responsibilities such as managing the farm. The early Christian attitude toward women reinforced the power of the patriarch, however.

Women were believed to represent the evils of sex and to be the unwholesome tempters of men. St. Paul, so significant in the reinstatement of men as elders in the tradition of Moses, feared women. He taught that women were tainted with the sin of Eve. Women were warned to confine themselves to housework and prayer. They were expected to unquestionably support the authority of the oldest male in the family. In time, women would begin to assert the equality of the sexes, but for most of recorded history, the male elder and the holy men have been the most dominant.

In primitive societies, old men enjoyed an enviable position in the clan. They possessed an air of supernatural prestige. He whose age brought him closer to the beyond was the best mediator between this world and the next. At the same time the "beyond" was also felt to be a domain of the forces of good and evil. Some old men and women were suspected of having evil associations and were even put to death because younger people feared their elders' netherworld cohorts. The supernatural prestige elder's enjoyed also had its dark side. People feared power gleaned from the unknown. This philosophy offers a glimmer of insight about the fundamental ambivalence toward old people that is still evident today.

An elder's familiarity with sacred concepts and myth combined with the experience and knowledge gained from long life increased their importance in the Old World, both east and west. These cultural attitudes were similar in all the great ancient civilizations. In China, as an example, eldership was believed to liberate people from the confinement of one's libidinal drives, set them free from the prison of collecting material possessions and promote them to the rank of living spirit. Greek philosopher Epicurus advised the elder to "live unknown" and be respectful of younger people's belief in their supernatural connection.

While elders were often felt to have special power, they were also seen to be physically feeble. They were understood to have long life experience but became decrepit. "Impotent, useless, he is also intercessor, magician, priest, beneath or beyond the human condition, and often both at once...a sub-human and a superman"[84] Primitive people feared old age just as much as twentieth century people do. Elders, who were usually the oldest citizens reminded people of their own mortality. The ambivalence was apparent, for example, in the premodern society's prayer that their king's would live into old age. There are many Babylonian and Egyptian invocations found in the Bible that move in this direction. Herodotus, the Greek historian, tells us of some tribes that worshipped their elders as gods and of others who ate them. At one extreme were the Issedones who gilded the heads of their parents and offered sacrifices to them. At the other were the Sardinian people who disposed of their old people by throwing them off a high cliff and laughed as they hit the rocks below.[85] Ancient people, therefore, had a mix of reactions to old people that left them ambivalent. Elders were respected for their many years of life but feared both because they had special powers and they reminded people of the reality of death.

Oral Tradition

Elders played a special role in maintaining a historical record of society. They carried a fund of valuable knowledge that was often confused with wisdom. The elder in these cultures transmitted knowledge he literally had to memorize. He educated the young by verbally passing on stories, myths and family memoirs. The elder's presumed wisdom and experience constituted one of society's most venerable institutions. This is one of the most striking contrasts primitive culture had with modern developed societies. The oral history passed on by the elders of early times was often very accurate despite the inclination elders had for occasional interpretation. This excerpt from G.I Gurdjieff's *Meetings With Remarkable Men* gives us one example of impact oral history had on one boy who lived in the nineteenth century. Gurdjieff relates this instance from his youth:

> One day I read in a certain magazine an article in which it was said that there had been found among the ruins of Babylon some tablets with inscriptions which scholars were certain were no less than four thousand years old. This magazine also printed the inscriptions and the deciphered text—it was the legend of the hero Gilgamesh.

> When I realized that here was that same legend which I had so often heard as a child from my father, and particularly when I read in the text the twenty-first song of the legend in almost the same form of exposition as in the songs and tales of my father, I experienced such an inner excitement that it was as if my whole future destiny depended on all this. And I was struck by the fact...that this legend had been handed down ...from generation to generation for thousands of years, *and yet had reached our day almost unchanged.*[86]

The old also enjoyed prestige because they were few in number in a slowly changing world where writing was rare. In an ancient elder's lifetime, his experience was never outdated. In ancient times people considered longevity a divine blessing. The Old Testament is full of references that show the eminence and dignity of the elders. Jeremiah was told by God, for example, to surround himself with elders for they were wiser than were the priests (Jeremiah 19:1, 26:17).

Old But Not Always Wise

There is also evidence, however, that not all old men were considered eminent. "Great men are not always wise." (Job 32:6-9). "Speak, old men, it is proper that you should, but know what you are talking about, and do not interrupt the music." (Ecclesiasticus 32:3-5). "The wise man's knowledge will increase like a flood and his advice is like a living spring, [however], the heart of a fool is like a broken jar, it will not hold any knowledge." (Ecclesiasticus 21:13-17). Older people were few in number in ancient times. This increased the visibility of the elder, if not his preeminence. An archeologist who studied longevity by assessment of prehistoric skeletons found that 95 percent of humans died before turning forty years of age.[87] No matter the life expectancy, there was always a group of people who were considered to be elders. The ancient cultures needed to believe in the power of the elder. Because the old in general were subjects of religious devotion, "respect for old age [was a] widespread occurrence [in primitive societies]. Some degree of prestige…seems to have been practically universal."[88]

There was also a stage of life beyond that of "elder." Those who reached it were treated with severity and little respect. While most primitive people honored their elders, they showed little mercy toward the extreme old, the senile or decrepit. The people of Samoa, for example, buried their elders alive if they lived to this "stage beyond eldership." Even the victim himself helped to organize the burial ceremony. In extreme old age people became useless in the eyes of the Jewish councils of elders because it was believed that old age caused poor judgement. In eleven of seventeen tribes in Israel, suicide was a frequent practice in this last stage of life.[89]

It was difficult in ancient civilizations to separate old people in general from elders. As the young decided which of the older citizens deserved their respect, they were likely overwhelmed by traditions that honored old age no matter how limited a elder's apparent pool of wisdom. Roman philosopher Cicero asserted that old people were honored only on condition that they defended themselves, maintained their rights, were subservient to no man and to the last breath ruled over their own domain. Cicero was not as concerned with elder wisdom as he was elder power. Seniority was honored even among the Greek gods, i.e.. *age before wisdom.* In the governments of Athens, Sparta and Rome, men spoke in order of age.

Chinese Eldership

Early communities of peoples of all races were structured around the tribe as a big extended family. It was the foundation of society. The most honored members of the tribe were visible and present throughout their lives because the tribes were relatively small. Whether the elders were parents, grandparents or more distant relatives, their influence could be felt and their support sought whenever needed. Since the civilized world from 0-1000 AD was no longer nomadic, extended family was within reach. In the Far East, for example, Chinese family structure was representative of most of Asia's cultures. Up until Communism became the driving force in the early twentieth century, the *tsu*, or clan "included all persons with a common surname tracing descent from a common ancestor. The *tsu* operated through a council of elders…" who usually implemented its will through the family's patriarch.[90]

Unlike the Israelites, the Chinese elder attained status most of all from the Confucian belief in ancestor worship. Older men were shown deference because they were the closest living contacts with one's ancestors. It was believed that after death a man's higher soul, the *hun*, became a mighty and beneficent deity. Participating in and drawing sustenance from the sacrifices offered in an ancestral temple by living descendents, the ancestor in turn guided and assisted his descendents. The fear that the *hun* would not be able to continue a good after-life, and thus become a miserable ghost without these signs of active worship, not only moved traditional Chinese to make sacrifices but also to continue the male line. Males were exalted over females because they were the only sex allowed to make sacrifices in the temple.

The other compelling virtue that led to the honoring of older people in China was the Confucian concept of filial piety: reverence and respect for family. Filial piety was both a moral and social virtue. When children practice respect for their parents, the Chinese expected that they would in turn love their siblings. When they accomplished this, they will hopefully love and respect all humans, thus acting out of their humanity, their *jen*. Confucius said *jen* is what makes us human and forms the foundation for all human relationships. Reverence for the elderly in China has often reached the extreme, as this news story from the early twentieth century demonstrates:

> A Chinese man aided by his wife, flogged his elder mother. The imperial order not only commanded that the criminals should be put to death; it further directed that the head of the clan should be put to death, that the immediate neighbors each receive eighty blows and be sent into exile; ...that the granduncle and uncle, and the two elder brothers should be put to death; that the prefect and rulers should for a time be deprived of their rank; that on the face of the mother of the father offender, four Chinese characters expressive of neglect of duty should be tattooed, and that she be exiled to a distant province; that the father of the female offender . a bachelor of arts, should not be allowed to take any higher literary degrees, and that he be flogged and exiled; that the son of the offenders should receive another name, and that the lands of the offenders for a time remain fallow.[91]

Indigenous History

Throughout the history of the great cultures of Europe, Asia and North America, numerous smaller "pre-civilized" societies have maintained elder traditions and accounts unlike those in more modern cultures. The man who would accept the mantle of eldership in the twenty-first century can learn a great deal by studying the elders of indigenous cultures. Indigenous people are the descendents of the original inhabitants of a given geographic territory. They generally possess a distinctive culture in which they have an ancient sense of place and an active relationship with the natural world. While "modern" man struggles with allowing elders to have a voice, traditional native knowledge about man pushes indigenous people toward admiration of and dependence on the word of the elders. These "primitive" societies still depend on oral history and education of the young by the adults, not by public schools. They remain agricultural and not nomadic, and small extended families are the norm.

The elder in indigenous society has a deep understanding of the interconnectedness of the universe. They assume that a force greater than themselves has caused the shared origin of all forms of life and the ecological integrity of natural systems.[92] They have a fearsome respect for the bonds of kinship between human beings and other living species. Domination of indigenous people by "modern" society over the past few centuries has left us with a devalued impression of native thought. Primitive people's views toward nature, medicine, relationships and religion are unjustly maligned as being to simple or naïve, and irrelevant to modern man's needs.

The most extraordinary elder in the ancient and present day indigenous cultures is the *shaman*. This traditional figure of authority is also known as the healer, medicine man or magician. This is not to say that others do not attain elder status. Indigenous people emulate shamanic ways whether expressed by the shaman or by other men. The shaman is like the senior elder who inherits the role of guardian of esoteric knowledge and is usually a technician of sacred power. The knowledge and belief systems of indigenous man and his medicine man has survived over thousands of years. It has worked for him and needed little evolution to be useful. The traditional behavior of the shaman is bizarre by Western standards and does not serve to make the native elder trusted by modern men.

In one primitive society known as the Caribs, for example, the novice shaman young must leave his home and go live with the *old peai* (i.e., shaman), who initiates him. The process of training and initiation can take ten years. The elder *peai* secludes himself in a hut where he whips the novice regularly, making him dance until he faints. The novice is bled by ants and is driven frantic by being forced to drink tobacco juice. He then "graduates" after going on an extended fast. In both the initiation of a shaman and in his own healing, there is a pattern of a recurring series of trances, symbolic death, voyages of his soul to other dimensions and, finally, an application of the knowledge acquired in the sacred world to a particular need such as healing or offering a blessing.[93]

In a review of both eldership and the process we go through to select our elders, indigenous knowledge is relevant to our spiritually and environmentally turbulent modern existence. Their magic may scare us or leave us dubious but it can work for modern man. Even though Western society and its scientists don't readily accept this, I believe we need the Native Mind. "We will always need the Native Mind's vibrant images of a living natural world that can penetrate to the deepest and most heartfelt…realms of human understanding."[94] Anthropologists believe, despite their cultural diversity, indigenous communities worldwide are bound together by a number of shared ecological and spiritual perspectives and themes which form a kind of universal consciousness that brings forth an extraordinary wisdom. These include:

1. Viewing nature as holy rather than simply temporal or wild
2. Believing that spirit is not the expression of one Supreme Being but is dispersed throughout the universe
3. Assuming human beings are responsible for sustaining harmony in nature and with man
4. Depending on natural cycles in time rather than progression caused by humans
5. Accepting that the universe possesses mysteries that will never be solved by humans
6. Tending to celebrate the orderly design of nature rather than dissecting it for the sake of science[95]

The indigenous man honors as his "most esteemed elders those individuals who have experienced a profound and compassionate reconciliation of outer and inner directed knowledge, rather than virtually anyone who has made material achievement or simply survived to chronological old age."[96] Indigenous man believes that all older people have something to teach the young. However, they are clear that only a few have the knowledge of the orderly and harmonious whole that is the universe. This knowledge, they believe, equips the mature and balanced elder to provide wise mentoring. The role of these true elders has traditionally been to facilitate rituals and provide support that assists people in becoming aware of themselves and their relationship to the Earth.

In native cultures as in modern, wisdom is found in those elders who experience life emotionally, that is, those who have compassion for and are responsive to others. The true indigenous elder is capable of initiating intimate, insightful and understanding relationships with people. They connect with nature at the same time and don't find the two separate. The relationship between eldership and old age has to be proven in the behavior of the indigenous elder as much as in modern Western cultures. "Naturally older craftsmen have more experience in their trades…but…their knowledge [may have] precious little to do with wisdom. Of what use are instructions and moral sermons if one's capacity for feeling and compassion has been lost?"[97]

In traditional cultures the function of the elder has not been limited to passing on concepts, but demonstrating the embodiment of knowledge. This awakens men and assists them in their intellectual and psychological growth simply because they are in the presence of a sage. The elder is there, they believe, to create conditions for an experience through which knowledge can be absorbed. Modern men describe these primitive elders as irrational and intuitive because the primitive elder's beliefs include the position that man's existence is a mystery and possesses dimensions that remain beyond human logic. Not only does the native elder believe that much of life's meaning is unexplainable, he believes that man's make-up cannot be analyzed piecemeal. The totality of existence is not a series of individual parts that can be dissected for study, but a whole in which parts are integrated and dependent upon one another.

The continued modernization of the world has created a larger and larger gap between modern and more "natural" ways of being. The decline of eldership and our Western suspicion of elders may have cut us off from the potential for maturity and balanced development. There has been a notable decline over the past 200 years in the importance of sacred ceremonialism and its role in helping men grow from one stage of life to another. The shaman, as representative of the people, sponsored the rites of passage. There is no evidence that a secularized urban world has lessened the need for ritualized expression of an individual's transition.

The Holy Men

Taoism in the Far East taught old people that old age was a virtue in itself. Taoism promised that aging took a man out of the confining shell of his own sensuality, to set him free from the material prison of his own possessions, and to promote him to the rank of a living spirit.[98]

In the Hindu world of today, a joint family system much like the tsu of China has survived centuries of East Indian history. The joint Hindu family is a cooperative at the head of which is the senior member of the family: usually male, but female if the patriarch has died. Often, the younger members of the family go to the family head and take dust from his or her feet as a token of their blessing. However, both the family head and the family priest share the elder role. The Hindu family priest is a man who has studied in and graduated from a seminary. He is an elder citizen who is devoted to the traditions of Hinduism, the predominant faith in India. He is a living expression of the tradition of the four *ashramas*—the four twenty-five year stages of life.

In the third stage, the one occurring between ages fifty and seventy-five years, a person begins detaching from family ties, acquired wealth and societal roles. This is in preparation for the 75- 100-year-old stage, the *sannyasa* ashrama. This final stage is most important to practicing priests who are devoted to service and self-realization. They are poor and supporting them is relatively simple for the family. The *sannyasin* eats little and desires little in the nature of clothing and other possessions. He is totally dependent on the support of others having given up ownership of nearly everything.

In India, China and other parts of the Far East, unlike in the West, the extended family remains the foundation of the community. However, even in these traditional cultures, a shift has taken place sometime in the past 2000 years that has caused the role of the elder to be split. In an upper middle class family in India, for example, there is a resident teacher and a priest sharing with the parents the responsibilities of educating the children. The teacher instructs the children both of the family and those of poorer families in the village. Therefore, the elder function of blessing is entrusted to the head of the family while the religious rituals are facilitated by the sannyasin. The education of the young is the responsibility of the resident teacher.

These three responsibilities—blessing, spiritual guidance and education—were originally assumed by parents. The elders of Moses' time assisted families in carrying out the tasks necessary to meeting these three responsibilities. Mothers and fathers allowed the elders to assist because these men were believed to be balanced and spiritual. They were wise men devoted to community first, and self, second. Even the sannyasin, who, in India, is admired as the ideal man who has renounced all worldly cares to attain the supreme goal of enlightenment, is self-selected. The ancient elder was honored and selected by the community. He was shown extraordinary deference by the young and without their blessing would have no role in the tribe.

Socrates

Beginning in ancient Greece, it was decreed that a person was first a member of the community and an individual second. Socrates, however, put forth the philosophy that the need for the approval of and participation in society should give way to individual conscience. The aim of the wise man, according to the great teacher, was no longer the plaudits of the masses, but self-sufficiency. To Socrates, "the wise man was not the one whose abilities had been expanded to fill his needs, but one whose needs had contracted to balance his abilities."[99] The route to self-sufficiency for him and his followers included a simplification of life much like that of the sannyasin.

Although Socrates is accepted more as a philosopher than a religious character, his principles had a significant impact on future holy men all over the world. Socrates said, "I think that to want nothing is to resemble the gods and that to want as little as possible is to make the nearest approach to the gods, that the Divine nature is perfection and that to be nearest to the Divine nature is to be nearest to perfection."[100] Those influenced by Socrates, including Diogenes, believed that enlightenment or salvation required a denial of wealth and indulgence. Holy men of the first few centuries AD were enamored with both Hindu and Greek theories of renunciation. This in turn led to a belief in the maxim that harsh conditions of living were more natural and more conducive "to morality and happiness than the sheltered existence of civilized people."[101]

Hermits

Among the Christians, a community of hermits who longed for salvation, began to form in Egypt and Syria around 400 AD. They have come to be called the Desert Fathers. These holy men left their families to seek redemption. They were not elders who had been selected by their people as in the case of Moses' people. They attained status because they risked their lives and renounced the trappings of civilized people in their quest for enlightenment. It was believed by many that clerics who were hermits and who devoted themselves to years of reflection and the renunciation of worldly goods were more likely to learn deep spiritual truths. Among the original Christians and the Russian Orthodox branch formed around 900 AD, the highest calling of the clergy was that of the hermit. In Russia the hermit-like clerics were called *staretz*.

By 1000 AD, culture had redefined the role of the elder from father, mentor, teacher, minister and source of blessing to hermit and ascetic. A devotee would have to go into the wilderness and seek out the hermit to take advantage of his wisdom. With the evolution of the professional clergy and in particular the solitary sannyasin, lama, desert priest or staretz, the concept of eldering shifted. Around the beginning of the second century, a change in family structure from extended kinship ties to a more nuclear family unit was evident in diverse cultures including Europe, Arabic Islam, sub-Saharan Africa, India, China and Japan. The combination of a professional clergy with a movement away from extended family left us with eldering functions spread among numerous people.

Decline of the Elder

"The vices of age were the vices of power—the greed and covetousness of economic power, the bullying and hectoring of political power...the arrogance of social power."[102]

Remember that a man is tempted away from the spirit by power. The elder in the early Christian era had a taste of power. Those who attained the status of elder were asked by the community to play a role in safeguarding and improving the prosperity of the tribe. The elders typically formed into councils whose leaders offered an opinion in all serious tribal matters. The council was also designated as a body of judges. In the Bible, elders are often described as being seated at the town gate acting as guarantors of the legal proceedings before them.

This evolution of the elder role is evident in the assembly of notables called the Sanhedrin, in Jerusalem. This elder body of seventy-one men with legislative responsibility was made up of scribes who did away with the need for oral traditions. They were priests who stepped in for the *pater familias*—the family's advocate for the sacred. The term elder acquired a different meaning in the first few centuries AD, because of the decline of the family patriarch's power from primitive times. In Greece, the authority of the central male figure began to diminish as early as 600 BC. The young had gained greater legal independence. For example, Athenian laws requiring respect for ones parents were consciously weakened.

First century Christian writers asserted that the authority of the *pater familias* was obliged to give way to divine authority. They taught that God was to be obeyed first, and parents second. The conversion of young people to the new religion formed to follow Jesus Christ was viewed by the pagan families as a rejection of family values. One of the Desert Fathers recorded this view on conversion: "But you say we must obey our parents. But whomsoever loves parents more than Christ loses his own soul."[103] Another tradition affecting mutual understanding between children and their fathers was the high incidence of female death in childbirth. The surviving husbands increasingly began marrying a second time and bore children by the second marriage. The age span between the father and his children was therefore greater in such marriages. So not only did conversion to Christianity erode the influence of the patriarch, age played a role as well. Many adult men had fathers whom they perceived as both old and frail.

The Challenge of Youth

The role of elder became splintered and begged the challenge of younger men. It is the nature of men to be in a position where they are protecting others. Sometimes men compete for this position. Young men who hoped to share the patriarch's position of power began to deride the elder. The young declared that wisdom was evident throughout their lifetime. They asserted that attaining wisdom was not dependent on reaching a certain age. The elder's longevity began to increase his culpability because he was around long enough to commit many errors. Old age was beginning to represent a defect in itself.

Philosophers such as Diogenes and Aristotle were very critical of older citizens who did not express eldership. Plato's attitude toward elders was respectful, which is understandable because he wrote much of his work between the ages of seventy and eighty. Aristotle, at age fifty, reported on prejudices in Greek culture that he found that were unfavorable towards the old. He wrote that Greek society looked upon its old as hesitant, suspicious, parsimonious, fearful, cowardly, selfish, pessimistic and avaricious.[104] Greek mythology always depicted older men as the enemy. The story of Uranus, castrated by his son Kronos, suggests that Kronos was justified in attacking the "elder" because Uranus' blood turned into evil giants when it flowed on the ground. Any old man with such evil in his bloodstream deserves confrontation and clearly he couldn't be a true elder.

The final generation of Olympian gods consisted of those who were either young or eternally in the prime of life. Homeric heroes were also young. Even the heroes who were older men such as Mentor, Odysseus' trusted friend, were honored because they were heroes and not because they were elderly. Homer's Aphrodite asserted that the gods hate old age. Both Greek tragedy and comedy scripts looked at the old as people who were in the way. The status of even the sages, therefore, must have been lower in ancient Greece than in the Hebraic world.

The lack of respect accorded older citizens was as troubling thousands of years ago as it is today. Even then, their potential as a resource to the young was underutilized. On the other hand, if the older person chooses not to utilize his long life experience to benefit others, does he encourage the respect of the community? In Greece more than in Israel, for example, history and myth tell us that older men attained high status if they participated in community affairs. If the old man was a judge, a priest, an arbitrator, a member of a council of elders or a teacher, the young Greek was more likely to hold him in high regard. This suggests that eldership had evolved into a call that mandated service. It was clear that the Greeks differentiated carefully between "old people" and "elders," with the latter demonstrating their passion through active participation in serving others.

By 100 AD or so, the Mediterranean world was reading the works of Plutarch, who integrated Roman values into his review of public affairs in the Greco-Roman world of the first century. He was clear on one point in particular—old men ought not to retire from political life. Plutarch taught that older men were diminished in libidinal stimulation like sex and lacked lively taste buds. As compensation for this depletion in "life instinct," he assumed that compensation could come from the pleasure of performing noble acts. "It is a man's duty not to allow his reputation to become withered in old age like an athlete's garland, but by adding constantly something new and fresh to arouse the sense of gratitude for his previous actions, and make it better and lasting."[105]

Plutarch recognized that the more the old monopolize power, the greater the impatience of the next generation. Throughout history the patriarch has provided an outlet for the accumulated resentment against old and oppressive fathers. The philosopher suggested, therefore, that elders not *seek* public office, but rather accept the appointment if offered. Plutarch foreshadowed Freud's concept of "thanatos," the death instinct. The death instinct pushes older people to address their mortality and contemplate what tasks need to be completed before their long life experience ends.

Thanatos energizes the elder like the libido energizes the young. Plutarch says old age's: "most grievous fault is to render the soul stale in its memories of the other world and make it cling tenaciously to this one...and to warp and cramp it, since it retains in this strong attachment the shape imposed upon it by the body.... Here old men especially go astray: once they have been drawn into admonishing others and rating unworthy habits and unwise acts, they magnify themselves as men who in the like circumstances have been prodigies of wisdom."[106]

The enmity of the young toward the old was especially understandable in the era when the family patriarch had power. The patriarch had absolute rights over all members of the family, including his wife. He could, with the authority of a modern juvenile court judge, punish a runaway. He could sell his children as slaves or exclude them from the family. Newborn babies could be abandoned on his order. After having conducted an inquiry and seeking the opinion of other family members, the patriarch could have a relative put to death without any interference from the local government.

Since in nearly all cultures the patriarch retained his power until death, it is not hard to imagine his offspring's resentment building over time. Roman comedies attracted an audience of young men because these plays commonly satirized the struggle between the young and the patriarch. The impact on respect for eldership was predictable. For the old it seemed that the more power they had, the more they were detested. Conversely, the greater their disenfranchisement, the more the young despised them.

A transition in patriarchal power began in the early part of the first century AD in Rome. From about 320 AD on, by public law, a father could no longer condemn his children to death. In part this was connected to the increasing influence of the mother. Under Roman law, a woman could become her children's guardian where the patriarch was absent. Emancipation of adult children became possible as well. The father's moral authority remained high, but he had less and less legal right to control the lives of his family members. In that *elders* and *patriarchs* were often the same person in early history, the declining respect for the patriarch influenced attitudes toward elders as well. Five forces led to the decline of the elder's influence:

1. The development of writing and the decline of a need for oral history
2. The formation of a body of professional clergy
3. The institutionalization of education of children
4. The growth of influence over the family of stratified society, bureaucracy and public law
5. Decreased respect for the male head of the family

As the teaching, blessing and nurturing elder roles were spread out among numerous players in increasingly more complex communities, the view of old people became more censorious. Just because a man had lived a long time didn't mean he had experienced life in depth. Most elders have used their long life experience to become more sophisticated and aware, while most of the *elderly* age without synthesizing wisdom from their experience. It became increasingly clear to younger generations which of the older men had depth, nurtured their souls and could energize others with their passion.

From the fifth to the tenth centuries, historians found little to praise about humanity. This was the time when the Roman Empire crumbled and the Christian church created a powerful infrastructure more driven by fear of losing power than by a devotion to sacred blessing. These were the Dark Ages, a time of war, robbery, famine and pestilence. This was an age in which elders may have been few in number, as the leadership of both governments and the church were preoccupied with survival. Art was only expressed through the making of spears, belts and jewelry. Writing was minimal and the writers had little confidence in the safety of their manuscripts.

Notable exceptions to the paucity of elders who lived in medieval times, however, were Charlemagne (emperor of the Holy Roman Empire), King Arthur of Britain and St. Augustine. It was Augustine who popularized the idea of true old age being the time between age sixty and 120 years and that the purpose of old age was the renewal of a man's spirit. He was careful to point out that living the Biblical life span of 120 years does not an elder make.

Wisdom

Possibly because there were few wise men in the Dark Ages, clarity came out of this time on the meaning of wisdom. As men waned in their expression of service and focused mostly on survival, a hunger grew for eldership's nurturing energy: *wisdom*. Coleridge said wisdom is "common sense in an uncommon degree." It is a flair of insight and intuition synthesized not through fear and doubt but through love and hope. The Buddhist says that the route to accessing wisdom has as its stepping stones *contemplation, listening, reflection and meditation.* These are also the behaviors of the balanced man in the second half of life.

The mind needs to be quiet to access wisdom, thus the need for the stepping stones. Eldership is wisdom in action. A man following a spiritual path who is lucky enough to be mentored by an older person is the recipient of elder wisdom. Wisdom need not be looked upon as something that is taught. "… for the seeker, wisdom is…indistinguishable from the pursuit of it."[107] We are seeking, in eldership, to "tap" our elder within and to synthesize from long life experience a common sense. Wisdom doesn't exist if it is not shared. The wise man hungers to share. The wise man is interested in his relationship to his neighbor, his family, to those who know him and depend on him but also to strangers. He wants to be accessible to those who like him but also to those who criticize him. He finds himself most alive when experiencing life among people with whom he can be a resource.

In their worship of gods and archetypes, the Greeks gave the name "Sophia" to wisdom. For them Sophia represented "divine" wisdom, the wisdom of the universe. Beginning with the archetypal seeker of wisdom, King Solomon, Sophia was felt to exude a feminine energy. "Wisdom is bright," said Solomon, "By those who love her she is readily seen…quick to anticipate those who desire her, she makes herself known to them." (Wisdom 6:12-14) When a *wisdomkeeper* expressed this energy it was believed to emanate from his Anima, the female energy in the psyche of a man. However, Sophia is also an expression of the balance of masculine and feminine energy in the psyche.

The Taoist tradition from China contains one of the oldest expressions of wisdom, focusing on the balance of *yin* and *yang*. Just as every child needs both father and mother in order to grow up in a balanced way, so every human being needs both the Divine Feminine (yin) and the Divine Masculine (yang) in order to mature. So wisdom, although felt by its first chroniclers to be feminine, is utilized by men only when it is expressed as a balance of masculine and feminine energy coming from the psyche and heated by spirit.

Wisdom as viewed by Buddhists is the expression of an enlightened person. A Buddhist who is on a spiritual path can seek to understand what is called "Buddha nature." A *Buddha* is any person who has completely awakened from ignorance and has opened to his vast potential of wisdom. This opening and the realizations that accompany it is "Buddha nature." Christians and Jews call this "God." Hindus call it the "self." Sufis call it the "Hidden Essence." Wisdom in the East includes the "wisdom of all-encompassing space," the womb of compassion. Wisdom is mirror-like. The wise man reflects back to others an accurate version of what they spoke, thus allowing them to review what they said. "Equalizing wisdom" is the lack of bias. The "wisdom of discernment" makes it possible to distinguish clearly without confusing different phenomena. The type of wisdom that is only reachable at death, the Buddhists say, is called "all-accomplishing wisdom."[108] These concepts about wisdom come largely from eastern traditions. There is some carry over in the West but our wisdomkeepers are very shy. Western men lack confidence that they have wisdom.

An elder is at minimum a wisdomkeeper. The wisdom he stores must be shared, but the wisdomkeeper only qualifies as an elder if the recipient of his wisdom is influenced by his knowledge and insight. In his review of medieval philosophers, including Origen and St. Ambrose, writer George Minois quotes them concerning eldership: "In Scripture, the name of elder...is...granted in order to honour maturity of judgement and gravity of life...Thus even in childhood there is a sort of venerable old age of behavior, and in old age a child-like innocence, because there is a form of old age which is venerable not by its duration, and which is not calculated by the number of years."[109]

In the Christian monasteries that appeared in the Middle Ages, leaders were selected based on their merits but also on the wisdom of their teaching. Even at the risk of disdain for the older monks, seniority was not a factor in the appointment of abbots. These professional Christians were not enamored of old age for its own sake. To them the "inner elder" has white hair. The inner elder was the energy they sought in their hunger for salvation and clarity about the meaning of life. Old age represented an abstract and symbolic problem of fallibility and depletion. The inner elder could be found in people of any age and represented both virtue and wisdom.

Christian philosophy in the Middle Ages included a spiritual purpose for aging. Although people of any age could tap inner elder energy, those persons over fifty or so were believed to have greater access to this energy. Aging was seen not simply as a process of moving from childhood to youth and maturity and then old age. Christian theologians acknowledged the possibility of transcending bodily age and reaching a more advanced spiritual age. Dante wrote that the "ennobled soul proceeds in due order [toward] its ultimate fruit." Medieval theologians assumed that spiritual development followed along with the body's aging process. Anglo-Saxon literature of the time shows a preference for the wisdom of old age over the innocence of youth. The concept of spiritual stages of life allowed for a paradoxical unity of physical decline and spiritual ascent.

In the Dark Ages the challenge of survival was great. It was not a time when even wise men could make much of a difference. It has been said that the function of an elder is a "linking together...a bringing into harmony...The sage is truly linked with the universe."[110] In medieval times, one-third of the population of Europe was killed by bubonic plague. In the wake of the plague, villages were abandoned, large amounts of land went untended and citizens revolted. The period from 1000 to 1500 AD was a time of constant war, rampages by bandits and mercenaries and the persecution of anyone who appeared unable to protect their means of survival. Large communities of people were discriminated against. Martyrs such as Joan of Arc paid a great price for standing up to the marauding hordes.

Wisdom is the due of the free. What the sage seeks is authentic freedom.[111] sixteenth century philosopher Michel Montaigne looking back from the glow of the Renaissance mused that "The chief sign of wisdom is a constant rejoicing...Its state is like that of things above the moon: always serene." It was not until the end of the Dark Ages that people once again were able to define the role of the elder and the meaning of wisdom.

The Renaissance

Recovery from the devastation of plague, war, pillage and pestilence in the Dark Ages took place in the sixteenth century. The process had an important effect on the credibility of the elder. The plague had focused its power on the young, thus leaving a disproportionate and larger number of older people in Europe. The survivors of the ravages of the Dark Ages regrouped to form extended families that provided protection for those left without. This led to the emergence of a gerontocracy: a society governed by the old. The older citizen was leading first families, then villages and then countries.

The elders would have been tempted to enter public service in the sixteenth century. An elder is devoted to the welfare of others and seeks opportunities to serve. Resistance and jealousy from the constituency usually accompanies a role in government however. The more an elder accepted important community responsibilities, the more they were seen as obstacles, or rivals, to be feared. Older men in authority were often subjects of criticism about their diminished ability to enjoy worldly pleasures. Renaissance writers and artists commonly illustrated the life span with twelve scenes, each representing a month of the year.

A man's potency and resiliency were shown to decrease beginning in the "fall" of his life. August corresponded to age forty-eight when youth was seen as coming to an end. This was *harvest time*. At age fifty-four, the end of September, the harvested grain is stored. It was believed that anyone entering the September of their life without financial means would be miserable and likely become a beggar. At age sixty, the end of October, old age set in. At the end of November at age sixty-six, a person shriveled up in preparation for death. And death was expected no later than age seventy-two. Old people, wise or not, were seen to be alone and living through a tragic time of life.

In the sixteenth century the Western world experienced a time of renewal called the Renaissance, in which youth was celebrated above all stages of life. Writers of fantasy began using the "fountain of youth" theme. Anything that suggested depletion or decline was hated and feared.

One poet wrote:

> *Many are the miseries of an old man*
> *Who seeks a fortune and fears to use it,*
> *Who seeks the future and fears to lose it,*
> *Who lacks courage, spirit, fire.*
> *He is slow, inert, quarrelsome, querulous,*
> *He celebrates the days of his youth*
> *And condemns the youth of others.*[112]

The Renaissance was a time of optimism and creativity, but aging ameliorated against this period's fantasy of eternal life. Medicine, magic and witchcraft searched for utopias and wellsprings of youth that could stave off old age and death. It is surprising that most of Shakespeare's classic "seven ages of man" were stages that occur between mid-life and very old age:

> All the world's a stage, And all the men and women merely players
> They have their exits and their entrances
> And one man in his time plays many parts
> His acts being seven stages. At first the **infant**,
> …And then the whining **school-boy**
> …And then the **lover**
> …Then a **soldier**
> …And then the **justice** …full of wise saws and modern instances
> …The sixth age shifts into the lean and slippered **pantaloon**
> …Last scene of all…is **second childishness** and mere oblivion
> …*Sans teeth, sans eyes, sans taste, sans everything.* (emphasis added)[113]

Unlike the elderly, elders are neither hungry for lost youth nor do they fear death. Eldership was, therefore, less visible in the people of the sixteenth century than at any other time in recorded history. The irrational and fear-based drive to avoid or outwit mortality was out of synchronization with the expression of eldership. The model for the Renaissance Man, the most sought-after condition was the *courtier*. This young, courteous, witty, brave and assertive swashbuckler was quite a contrast to the wise, patient and contemplative sage or elder. Wisdom was believed to be a quality that belonged to the old, yet old age was feared and jeered.

The Renaissance was a time of revolt against medieval religious authority and church platitudes. Preeminent among the Humanists who led the revolt and spread the revival of classical learning was Erasmus. He demonstrated the ambivalence among scholars about wise men:

> Increasing age brings…men wisdom, but they grow more and more foolish the nearer they approach old age. At the same time there's no people so cheerful…or so little affected by the misery of growing old…Imagine some paragon of wisdom to be set up against him, a man who has frittered away his boyhood and youth in acquiring learning…There you have a splendid picture of a wise man.[114]

The Renaissance was the beginning of "modern history." H.G. Wells wrote that people in Europe began in this era to actualize a personal will encouraged in part by the widespread development of schools. Literature, news and other forms of knowledge were becoming accessible to the common man. Wells wrote: "The ideal community towards which we move is not a community of will simply; it is a community of knowledge and will, replacing a community of faith and obedience" common during the Dark Ages.[115] The elder of more ancient times could engender respect through the demonstrated use of intuition, sensitivity and patience. But, in the sixteenth century and for centuries to come the elder would also be expected to be educated and knowledgeable. To mentor or to act as a steward of life required that a person know about the nature of man. According to Wells, by the time of the Renaissance, man was an informed being.

The Church

The Reformation of the Catholic Church that was sparked by such men as Martin Luther and John Calvin, brought a focus to the spiritual nature of eldership. Good works were no longer believed to be a series of pious acts designed to secure salvation. Service to man and community was seen as a manifestation of an inner conviction about one's spirituality.

In the medieval world, a man's eternal fate was determined by a priest's blessing, especially at the last moment of a person's life. John Donne declared in 1628, however, that "our critical day is not the very day of our death but the whole course of our life." [116] The whole of a man's life became important. Stewardship and service exemplify eldership. Martin Luther was highly critical of retirement from active life at any age. To him and his followers the purpose of existence was to utilize physical and intellectual strength to serve others throughout your life. This is what led to salvation.

Out of this era came a growing focus on the potential of the individual and less of a reliance on hierarchical authority and the priests of the church. The imitation of Christ like behavior led Christians to believe that an individual grows constantly toward the stature of God. This enhanced the view that spiritual growth is a continuous process of change or progression toward a more full life. Elders assume that this growth continues throughout your life. The Renaissance view of the world spread to the New World in the seventeenth century. From this time forward, the history of eldership was a Western World history taking in North America and Europe.

Modern History

In chapters one and two we reviewed the impact of eighteenth and nineteenth century industrialization on the family, on men and women and on older people. This was the time when the village and extended family began to break up. The impact of going to work in factories in urban areas of Europe and the USA changed the experience of families. The "enclosure" of men was the "historical process by which a people are separated from their ancestral work and land..."[117] Industrialization enclosed men into the cities and enclosed women into the home resulting in an imbalance in the full expression of mature masculinity and femininity. All of a man's

> auxiliary resources were taken from him, and he was now a wage earner and nothing more. Enclosure had robbed him of the strip that he tilled, of the cow that he kept on the village pasture, of the fuel he picked up in the woods and the turf of the commons...

They had lost their gardens …In their work they had no sense of ownership …The sense of sympathy and comradeship… the old village had been destroyed.[118]

With the movement of men away from the village came mobility for people in general. The pre-industrial rural community contained few travelers. You would typically find families in villages of the eighteen hundreds and earlier with roots that went back for generations.

The elder was accessible in the less mobile pre-industrial community. Grandparents, ministers, master craftsmen and older people in general could be sought out and found fairly easily by the young. The highly mobile twenty-first century elder is out of reach of the young. When I was giving a talk on eldering at a Unitarian Church in Oregon City, Oregon, a young father said, "We would like to take advantage of the wisdom of elders, but they are leaving us in the dust of their RVs!" The rich source of wisdom called *common sense* has become more difficult to tap as families and communities began to spread out. Philosopher Gabriel Marcel lamented, "There is and there can be no common sense where there is no common life or common notions, that is to say where there no longer exist any organic groups such as the family, the village and so on."[119] The interplay between elders and the young is considerable in settled, non-nomadic, relatively isolated rural communities. There was "folklore to be guarded and handed down, and there is religious thought, cosmic ceremony and rites de passage" facilitated by elders in small communities.[120] This brings them honor and motivates them to serve.

As men changed their work focus from subsistence to wage earning and women were forced to take on more domestic duty to compensate for father absence, the elder's credibility shifted. The attitude of the young toward the old in general shifted away from automatic veneration, to the equality of people of different ages, and in time to the exaltation of youth. Our modern bias toward the ages of man is that the great challenges of growth occur before the age of fifty. Western man has forgotten that personal growth is possible even after mid-life. With a shift in our attitudes toward aging we usually find a shift in our attitudes toward the sage's and wise men as well.

Indications of the shift toward gerontophobia, the fear of old age, include a sharp decline around 1800 in the use of grandparents names for offspring. The abolition of meeting-hall seating preferences for the elder began about the same time. The first mandatory old age retirement laws were passed in the United States between 1777 and 1818. Laws structuring inheritance of property and the descent of names appeared in New England at the beginning of the nineteenth century. In some respects the Revolutionary War in the United States (1776) and the French Revolution (1789) can be viewed as revolutions of the young directed at a gerontacracy: an oligarchy of the senior citizen.

The next great Western event that impacted elders was immigration. The older generation of Europeans and Asians either were left behind in their native countries or emigrated to the USA, Canada and South America where they were less able to mentor and model survival skills. Generational conflict was common among the immigrants who settled in North and South America. Immigrant children adjusted to life in the new land more easily than did the adults. The young felt less attached to European traditions and picked up the new language more readily. Children began to complain about the elder's "old country" way of thinking. Where in Europe the elders modeled functional ways of thinking, in the new land they were seen as unskilled. Family heritage was not as meaningful to the young who wanted to become like the Americans or Canadians. The family heritage of the immigrants was largely rural. In America, however, immigrant families of the late 1800s were not only drawn to farmland but to the jobs in the urban areas. Cities, meanwhile, had been expanded, fueled by the growth of industrialization. Mills and factories were hiring thousands of unskilled workers.

The final great blow to the hearts of elder men was World War I and World War II. On the fighting fronts the USA suffered 291,000 killed and 670,000 wounded. When I urge my father to talk about the events of his life, his greatest resistance shows when it comes to the years of WWII. He fought in the Pacific. He saw death. He can't think of a way to describe the abomination of war. It is evident that the War had a permanent impact on his soul. Our fathers didn't feel good about themselves as soldiers because they were not archetypal warriors. They were extensions of war machines and killed with guns that are dishonorable weapons. To kill with the sword, the honorable warrior of earlier times had to confront his enemy, see him, feel his heat. The warriors of WWII killed a distant enemy who was faceless. Their spirits died of the shame of mass murder.

At home there were even greater losses. The rush to churn out planes and tanks contributed to work related accidents that killed nearly 300,000 workers and disabled one million more. WWII reversed a trend of moving toward greater job safety that had gathered speed in the 1930s. As the soldiers lived in constant fear of death, homebound loved ones were facing occupational risks daily.

This chapter was a review of how the role of elder has evolved. In the next chapter we will look at eldership as an expression that can fit our modern view of men's roles. Men's expression of mature masculinity has changed from era to era and from culture to culture. Eldership, however, is universal. The meaning of eldership has remained the same throughout time and in all history elders have attempted to be stewards of mature masculinity. They have accomplished this through blessing, mentoring and through initiation. Next we will consider the New Male and his expression of eldership.

❖   ❖   ❖   ❖

Harry, an elder with over 80 years life experience

Wisdom has something to do with devotion. Devotion to doing something with purpose and devoting yourself to others.

One of the oldest elders I have met is Harry. He is somewhere in his eighties but he isn't telling. Harry was, for many years, a mental health professional. Highly trusted, he had studied his art so well that he was able to integrate both intuition and science into his counseling work. This made him "right" a great deal more often than most of us hoped to be as he counseled people with marital problems, emotional distress or alcoholism. A number of years before I met him he had retired from doing counseling and was devoting his time to mentoring young people at a few nearby community theatres. He also cared for his vineyard where he reported that, "he found his footing" He was an expert in acting and directed numerous plays and musicals. His artistic ability included creating a farm from scratch and specializing in raising grapes in the challenging environs of Northwest Oregon.

As he sat with me listening to my ideas for a book on elders, we discussed whether wisdom was a prerequisite for eldership. Harry did not consider himself wise. He felt comfortable being who he was, loving what he enjoyed and trying to avoid judging others. He was filled with wisdom but he was shy of being labeled wise. Harry's wife had passed away in the recent past. She was the wise one he told me. It was from her that he learned what a meaningful life was. "It has to do with devotion," he said, "Devoting yourself to creating something that gives you a sense of purpose, devoting yourself to loving others and devoting yourself to being accessible to the young."

Chapter IV

ELDERS AND THE NEW MALE

Fathers, lovers of different kinds,
Share my dream
Giving me a ride to maturity.
Deeply male, balanced man
I am drawn to be
By spirit-centered celebration.

Taking a break from the family gathering, two men walked slowly through the park. The younger man said, "Ilene and I are going to get an apartment together."

The older man started at Josh's announcement. He took a deep breath and then offered a small smile.

Josh spoke again, saying, "We are going to try living as a couple before committing to marriage." He waited for a reaction from Dean, the older man, because he trusted and respected him.

Dean knew that Josh wanted a response. He finally spoke. "When I discovered I was in love with Linda, I wanted to marry her," thinking back on the day he realized he had fallen in love with his wife.

"It was less common for couples to live together before marriage in your day, wasn't it?" asked Josh.

"Yes," said Dean. "But, it wasn't convention that drew me to marry her. I couldn't resist. I needed to live with her forever."

97

Josh stopped walking, looked into his uncle's eyes and said, "I wish I were as sure about Ilene and me. How do you know when you are ready for a commitment like yours?"

The older man reached out and touched the younger man's shoulder. He found he needed another deep breath. Many thoughts, memories and theories rushed through his mind. He felt the weight of Josh's question and wanted to be wise for him. He could offer so many opinions about love, commitment, cohabitating versus marriage. His intuition told him, however, that his role was to be available for Josh, focused and supportive. This young man had placed Dean in the important role of mentor. He could escape the responsibility or give his all as a listener, wisdomkeeper and source of nurture. Dean might even ask Josh some questions that would help his young mentee find his own answers.

Like the archetypal elder, Socrates, Dean realized that asking a few good questions would lead a mentee to recognize the truth from *within himself.* Socrates believed the answer created by the student came from within him "from a store of truth, which it [the student] already possesses unconsciously."[121] Socrates also had considerable experience in mentoring. Dean was older and more experienced than Josh, but he wasn't sure he was being called upon to do much more than listen. He did know that the younger man would create his own answer once ready.

The *elder* has wisdom. This means he is more than knowledgeable. The elder has confidence in his intuition and is, therefore, able to discern what is most right or closest to true for the circumstance in that time and place. But even more important than demonstrating discernment, the elder is a *sage* whose sensitivity and maturity leads him to behave in such a way that the student is more likely to find his own solutions within.

When the elder takes the time to be present for a younger man, as did Dean, he does so in part to experience the quiescence of giving. Following this instinct requires that he be accessible. Being present means that the older person *holds the container* for the younger. Holding the container is a quiet, contemplative duty defined by psychoanalyst, Carl Jung. The man who holds the container is expressing unconditional positive regard for the other as he focuses on the mentee, bringing the energy of the universe to the place where the two of them meet. The picture you get is of the elder holding a giant ball of light that surrounds the young he holds dear. The light brings warmth, an air of patience and support.

Just as the energy of the libido swings us into a tumult of activity expressed outwardly, thanatos energies of equal force press inward on older people toward quieting and soul-nourishing equilibrium. You will recall that thanatos is the instinctual life force driving us in the second half of life. It longs to return to a state of peace. These inward moving forces drive the elder as he peacefully stands by while a pupil grows or, at least experiences, a moment of confidence because of the advocacy of the teacher. Martin Buber says it beautifully:

> The teacher helps his disciples find themselves, and in hours of desolation the disciples help their teacher find himself again. The teacher kindles the souls of his disciples and they surround him, his life with the flame he has kindled. The disciple asks, and by his manner of asking unconsciously evokes a reply, which his teacher's spirit would not have produced without the stimulus of the question.[122]

Eldering, more than teaching, has the potential of providing the young access to a *mature* expression of self that fits the way we live today. Elders respect the knowledge that the young hold. Margaret Mead witnessed that in most cultures, both primitive and modern, there were three stages of development for the mature elder. Children listen to and learn from their elders. In young adulthood, we find stimulation and learning through observing our peers. And then, in later life, if we are balanced, we listen to the young. The elder, unlike the elderly, thrives on facilitating the takeover by the young for they inherit the earth.

The elder male is not only an advocate for the young but believes that advocacy for men means being aware of a new psychology for men. In this book I call this mind-set *mature masculinity*: a concept of masculinity that honors archetypal maleness while at the same time accepting the reality of modern-day western society. This has resulted in new gender roles for men and women. Mature masculinity does not incorporate the juvenile or underdeveloped aspects called *traditional masculinity,* such as the devaluation of women. Traditional masculinity is the unfortunate but predictable result of the male role socialization process beginning with the Industrial Revolution.

Twenty-first Century

In the eighteenth century men were in a position of prominence in the home and in the community. Little had changed in the historical view of what was traditional masculinity. In the nineteenth century, however, the industrialization of culture began a massive change in men's roles. As men moved increasingly "off the farm" and into the city to become a cog in the new "machine era" they left the nuclear family. Fathers were moving away from the home, from their children and essentially left a void in the family that women were forced to fill. The family home became more feminized as masculine energy became less available. "Masculinity came to be defined less in terms of self-control and family obligation…and more in terms of competition, ambition, assertiveness and virility."[123] These became core aspects of the masculine mystique we discussed in chapter two.

In the latter part of the last century, women led us through a redefinition of femininity that has impacted masculinity. Given our focus on feminism, men and women alike have lost track of what mature masculinity really means. Warren Farrell writes in *The Myth of Male Power,* "Have we been misled by feminists? Yes. Is it feminist's fault? No. Why not? Men have not spoken up. Simply stated, women cannot hear what men do not say. Now men must take responsibility to say what they want—to turn a 'War in Which Only One Side Shows Up' into a 'Dialogue in Which Both Sexes Speak Up.'"[124]

During the twentieth century the potential has arisen for a new model of male and female behavior and interaction. Within this generation, social change has escalated. In the 1960s, the sexual revolution, the peace movement, the civil rights movement and the women's movement occurred. In questioning old ways concerning our sex life, imperialism, our treatment of minorities and the status of women, we introduced a more expansive human relations ethic that has redefined men's approach to women and visa versa. "Only then did self-esteem become accepted as essential to women's and men's health which was redefined to include psychological and spiritual health as well as physical health."[125] Then, very suddenly, in the 1970s people began looking inward for answers. It was as if the high energy of the 1960s broke down our barriers to introspection. Many people turned to psychotherapists, spiritual guides and other personal growth gurus. Then came the self-indulgent, narcissistic 1980s. We rushed headlong toward finding wealth and speeded up our technological development to make life more comfortable, without thinking through the consequences. In the 1990s, there was evolution in the air and hope that the next century would bring balance to men and women. In the twentieth century, we redefined gender roles, challenged the masculine and feminine mystique and brought more, but not total equality to the sexes.

Still, we have not moved far enough. As the twenty-first century dawns, we must explore the possibilities for a new expression of masculinity. Men need to grasp the new meaning: that archetypal masculinity has been modified by culture and its modern expression demands new behaviors…behaviors one can witness in the expression of *mature masculinity.* Men must also reach out to women and take the risk that both genders can build a connection that honors gender equality and can infuse life back into the nuclear family. Fathers must have hope that they will play an active role in raising their children. And women must have faith that they can trust the "new male."

For thousands of years, the three basic male roles have been protector, provider and teacher of cultural tradition. The provider of the twenty-first century has more complex skills than the hunter and gatherer of earlier times. Men used to be the primary source of the family's food and shelter. Today, men and women both provide. Men retain a drive to be a provider, but have fewer outlets for this passion. Today, we have institutions such as police, fire and social welfare departments that are set up to protect our families. To teach our children we have created complex school systems. Men and women have joined energies and talents to provide, protect and teach.

To speculate about what a twenty-first century expression of masculinity might look like, let's consider a new look at the three male role prescriptions. Remember to prepare for eldership, men must seek to become balanced socially, psychologically, physically and spiritually. It is likely, therefore, that a man can accomplish this balancing in part by understanding and expressing in a modern way the roles of protector, provider and teacher. Consider these new versions:

Protector:

- Being accessible to and supportive of one's family and not separate from his spouse and children
- Being a conservationist rather than a exploiter of the Earth
- Standing up for ideals, beliefs or standards that will protect children and encourage them to care for themselves
- Standing up for the equal rights of men and women
- Perpetuating nonviolence and nondiscrimination
- Endeavoring to make the relationship with the mother of his children endure and grow

Provider:

- For fathers, committing to share parenting and honoring the different skills of each parent
- Seeking to find his passion and following it—this is the opposite of seeking wealth for its own sake
- Becoming aware of personal power—this is the opposite of seeking power in order to dominate.
- Taking care of health: physical and mental (Those who depend on you will get the best opportunity to experience your advocacy.)

Teacher:

- Bringing to the family information about how to survive in the world
- Being a "spiritual elder" in the second half of life
- Initiating his children into adulthood
- Sponsoring the process of introducing his children to the extended family and work towards building a family tradition of keeping the extended family connected
- Assessing who in the marriage is best suited to work and who is best suited to care for the home and those at home

Archetypal Masculinity

Before looking at the new expression of these three roles, let's review the original meaning of each. A model for masculine and feminine expression can be found in pre-modern symbols, which form images. Carl Jung popularized the concept of premodern symbols having psychological meanings. He called these symbols *archetypes.* He went further, however, to say the images created by the archetypes can be identified in people by patterns of behavior. People behave in predictable ways, he suggested, because imprints in the psyche govern the way we act. In other words, men and women are "hardwired" to express themselves in patterns of behavior we call masculine or feminine. The psyche is all of the human being that is not physical: is the emotional, psychological and spiritual processes, conscious and unconscious, that make up the human personality.

Jung said that our psychological processes originate in a community psyche he called the *collective unconscious.* The collective unconscious is a single consciousness made up of all our psyches connected by energy Jung felt was spiritual in nature. The worldwide memories and experiences of humans are accessible in the collective unconscious. The history of man is found there also. So the archetypes are common, repeated images that go all the way back in time and exist across all world cultures. Physical characteristics reaching back to primitive life forms are inherited. Jung said this is also true for our universal, archetypal memory. It is inherited in the form of energies or behaviors.

An example of an archetype is the elder. When Jungian analysts such as Dr. Allan Chinen discuss mature behavior, they refer to the "elder within." This is the *energy* within the psyche that influences Elder-like behavior. Chinen contrasts the popular archetype, Hero, with the elder. Our image of the Hero is someone who rides in and saves the victim or captures a great treasure. The elder, writes Chinen, unlike the Hero, "does not leave his or her dismal situation seeking better fortunes. Instead, fortune comes to him, in the middle of ordinary, everyday chores, and the elder's task is to be open to this unexpected magic."[126] Here he is describing a common theme in old myths. It is in the stories passed down from our ancestors that one finds ancient archetypes described.

Jung studied myths, folklore and art in cultures all over the world. He found commonality. He based his theory also on a study of comparative religion and an analysis of dreams, fantasies and pictures produced by people he treated who came from all around the world.

Cultural anthropologists have catalogued a number of human traits common to all societies. All societies, for example, have laws about marriage. Ceremonies of initiation of young men are also found almost everywhere. Beliefs in the supernatural and soul concepts are universal. "If there is no human nature," wrote anthropologist Robin Fox, "any social system is as good as any other, since there is no base line of human needs by which to judge them. If…everything is learned, then surely men can be taught to live in any kind of society."[127] While culture can amend the way we express archetypal energies, there is a basic, enduring human nature. Protector, provider and teacher are universal masculine expressions that no man can ignore, but they have appeared different at various times in history. A hunger is hard-wired into the psyche of men that drives us to protect, provide and mentor or teach. The true nature of men and women speaks to us subtlety through stories, myths and even dreams. When this phenomenon collectively regarded as the *unconscious* speaks to us from inside, it often appears as a god, a symbol, a monster or a vision of a man or woman. The unconscious, unlike consciousness, is a phenomenon of memory. It doesn't belong to the present. It is our history speaking in symbols.

There are some common archetypes representing masculinity. They include the Elder, the Father, the King, the Prince, the Lover, the Warrior, the Wise Man, the Magician, the Priest and others. Another version of these are the ones proposed by Jungian analyst, E.C. Whitmont.[128] He called them Father, Son, Hero and Wise Man. He builds his archetypes from the Taoist concepts of Yin and Yang, the feminine and masculine principles, which the Chinese believed permeated the psyches of both men and women. Yang is assertive and initiating. Yin is passive and containing. Yin gives form, like gestation, to the energy of Yang.

The female archetypes used most commonly are Mother, Princess or Love Goddess, Amazon, and Priestess or Medium. The qualities of each of the four are comparable to those of the four male archetypes.

The Father and Mother are parental, protective and nurturing. The Prince and Princess are childlike, innocent and loving. The Hero and Amazon are strong and assertive. The Wise Man and Priestess are the mouthpieces of inner thought and wisdom. These four archetypes, with which each of us is born, guide us through the our natural life-cycle—being mothered, being fathered, exploring the world around us, connecting to our peers, growing through adolescence, being initiated, establishing ourselves in society, dating, making a family, earning an income, participating in religious rituals, assuming the responsibilities of eldership, and preparing for death.

The Father is the figure of authority and stands up for social order. This energy is also known in our stories and dreams as the King or Lord who directs and protects. The Father relates to others as children or subjects, not individual persons. This archetype is a steward of life and is procreative.

The Prince is forever an adolescent, with energy that is emotional and actively spiritual. This archetype is a seeker, preoccupied with his play and adventure. The Prince "goes his own way, seeks individual relationships and his own individuality, his own inner treasure, in ever new settings…"[129]

The Hero is the courageous, ambitious aspect of self, with energy that stirs devotion to some philosophy, ruler or country. The aggressive Hero, unlike the Father, is unconcerned with maintaining the status quo. This archetype will overthrow others if necessary in order to achieve his lofty goals.

The Wise Man is concerned with knowledge and ideas rather than personalities or emotions. This energy manipulates and plays others to teach a lesson. It embodies the intellect and its rational nature. It is not representative of eldership, however, although elders are often called wise.

These archetypes, which are models of masculine expression, can be found throughout literature. One of the best sources is in myths and fairy tales. King Arthur is one of the best models for the Father or King. Robin Williams, in the movie *The Fisher King,* plays a childlike and adventurous fellow who is a good example of the Prince archetype. The Samurai soldier found in stories of old Japan is an excellent model for the Warrior devoted to his master even at the risk of his own life. Merlin the Magician, who served King Arthur, was an archetypal Wise Man. Some good examples of the four archetypes are found throughout the three books of J.R.R. Tolkein's trilogy, *The Lord of the Rings.* Tolkien was one of our most modern writers of myth. In Tolkien's third book, *The Return of the King,* Gandalf, the author's version of the Wise Man, is in a discussion with Aragorn, a King:

In this excerpt, Gandalf counsels the King and encourages Aragorn to act like an archetypal King.

"…and Gandalf said: this is your rhelm and the heart of the greater rhelm that shall be…and it is your task to order its beginning, and preserve what may be preserved."

"I know it well, dear friend," said Aragorn "but I would still have your counsel."

In the following excerpt, Aragorn is shown to be generative, a steward of the earth. He exudes vitality, which are all kingly energies.

Then Aragorn laid his hand gently to the sapling and lo! It seemed to hold only lightly to the earth, and it was removed without hurt and Aragorn bear it back to the Citadel…And Aragorn planted the new tree in the court by the fountain and swiftly and gladly it began to grow.

The Wise Man archetype uses magic or what appears to be magic because of his powerful and unusual insight. In this excerpt, Gandalf is shown to be a magician who appears to have great power. His power, however, could be nothing more than illusion wise men can create with intuition and ken.

He raised his staff. There was a roll of thunder. The sunlight was blotted out from the eastern windows; the whole hall became suddenly dark as night. The fire faded to sullen embers. Only Gandalf could be seen, standing white and tall before the blackened hearth.

Tolkein depicts the Prince in the person of the Hobbit, Sam Gamgee. In this excerpt Gandalf comes upon little Sam eavesdropping.

"How long have you been eavesdropping?" said Gandalf.

"Eavesdropping, sir? said Sam. "I don't follow you, begging your pardon. There ain't no eaves at Bag End, and that's a fact."

"Don't be a fool! What have you heard, and why did you listen?" Gandalf's eyes flashed.

"Mr. Frodo, sir!" cried Sam quaking. "Don't let him hurt me, sir! Don't let him turn me into anything unnatural! My old dad would take on so. I meant no harm, on my honour sir!"

Gandalf and Frodo continued to press Sam for a response.

"I listened because I couldn't help myself, if you know what I mean. Lor bless me sir, but I do love tales of that sort. And I believe them too..."

Sam represents the childlike, playful self. He is passionate, impetuous and is not always in control of his need for stimulation. The Prince archetype is emotional and irrational.

Finally, the Warrior is found in the character of Boromir. This knight is driven by a need to protect and defend.

Boromir says,

"I was afraid for you, Frodo. If Aragorn is right and Orcs are near, then none of us should wander alone...Are you sure that you do not suffer needlessly?" he said. "I wish to help you. You need counsel...Will you not take mine?"

"I think I know already what counsel you would give, Boromir," said Frodo. "And it would seem like wisdom but for the warning of my heart."

Frodo is careful not to do all that Boromir suggests. He knows the knight is brave but he is dangerous as well. Boromir responds sharply to Frodo saying,

"Warning? Warning against what?"

"Against delay," said Frodo. "Against the way that seems easier."

Boromir responds,

"We shall fall in battle valiantly.... True hearted men, they will not be corrupted. We of Minus Tirith have been staunch through long years of trial."

Here, Boromir displays his sense of commitment to something outside of himself—to fall in battle if need be for the glory of his King. He is proud of his high level of military skill and physical strength.

To explore both cultural and archetypal masculinity, it will be beneficial to select archetypes that are as representative of worldwide and historical masculinity as possible, and from there, integrate the twenty-first century expression of masculinity. To develop a new expression of male roles functional in the twenty-first century, one must make two leaps of faith:

1. Accept that culture has a profound effect on the way we play our gender roles;
2. Accept that the basic meaning of masculinity or femininity is hard-wired into our psyche and is affected very little by culture.

King, Lover, Warrior, Magician

The four models of masculinity mentioned above, Father, Prince, Warrior and Wise Man, have evolved among men involved in men's growth into the four archetypes: King; Lover; Warrior; Magician (KLWM). The four are very much like the Father, Prince, Warrior and Wise Man. Writers such as Robert Moore and Douglas Gillette have synthesized a flavor of mature masculinity from the many names for masculine archetypes in the renaming of the archetypes into King, Lover, Warrior and Magician.

As I address the question, "What is an elder?" one answer is that the elder is a good example of how the four archetypes of mature masculinity look when expressed from the heart of a man who has considerable life experience. If a man experiences a balance of energy from each of the four archetypes—King, Lover, Warrior, Magician—he is approaching the expression of mature masculinity. Understanding the archetypes of masculinity gives him a blueprint for the fullest, most mature expression of what it means to express mature masculinity.

As we review the nature of the four archetypes of masculinity, KLWM, it is important to integrate the role of our "dark side." The expression of each archetype has a light and a dark side. The dark side is called the *shadow*. Becoming all that man can be requires identifying and controlling the shadow. Certain aspects of the "self" must remain inactive and held in the unconscious. These dangerous aspects are our shadow. When the shadow is directing our actions we are dangerous to others and ourselves. A life run by the shadow is evident in behaviors like addiction, uncontrolled anger, jealousy, fear and the exploitation of other people. It is the shadow that allows us to kill, justify our savage acts and model immaturity for the young to emulate. The balancing needed in mature masculinity is not only among the four archetypes but also between the "bright" energy of our psyche and the shadow energy of our psyche. We express energy from the functional bright side of the four archetypes but also from the shadow side. The King, for example, can be a tyrant as well as a generative leader. But a man who expresses Lover, Warrior and Magician energy as well harmonizes the energy of the King. This can act to quell the dark side of the King's energy.

To complicate this just a bit further, there are archetypes of "immature masculinity" as well. There are archetypes for boyhood as well as manhood. So we add a third step in utilizing the KLWM archetypes to describe grown-up men—that is to not confuse boy psychology with man psychology. Moderated but also enriched by life's experiences, boyhood archetypes give rise to manhood archetypes if you mature. In the growth process the grown-up man doesn't lose his boyish qualities.

The boyhood archetypes don't disappear. "The mature man transcends the masculine powers of boyhood, building upon them rather than demolishing them."[130] Moore and Gillette proposed that an impoverishment of men has resulted from stunted growth. The patriarchal, angry, detached, abusive men are boys pretending to be men. "They got that way honestly, because nobody showed them what a mature man is like."[131]

The man archetypes have the capacity to initiate, control and mediate the behavior of men. This is so even though we are fairly unaware of the archetypal energies. Before we look more closely at KLWM, one final comment about archetypes: they are not simply intellectual concepts. They have a feeling to them and are, therefore, hard to grasp intellectually. Ultimately you can't explain archetypal energy any more than you can explain how an emotion feels. You can experience it and you can describe the experience.

King

As we review the energy of the King archetype, keep in mind we are considering a model for the expression of masculinity that is based on instinctual traits "and their response to, as well as influence upon, those traits shaped by environment and culture."[132] In history, good kings included King David, Gandhi and President Kennedy. These real life models were not perfect but expressed "good king" energy often enough to be remembered for leadership and as a defender of social order, both of which are energies of the archetype. The king is the archetypal leader and the voice of the people. Although we are describing a form of energy from the psyche when discussing archetypes, I will refer to each as "he" just to simplify. The king directs and protects, heals and invigorates. The king celebrates life and is, therefore, generating life. He remains centered, bringing order to those around him, much like a straight spine facilitates good posture. The king can be considered idealistic or even naïve in his confidence and joyful spirit.

Two functions of the king are essential to growth from boyhood to manhood: these are *ordering* and *blessing*. Within the arena of his influence are creation and organization. Ordering is placing things in a proper and reasonable sequence. With ordering and blessing comes a kind of spiritual creation. Mythologist Mircea Eliade wrote that creation in ancient times was symbolized by a central force that radiated power. Pre-modern people found a center to their land where stood a tree or a mountain and often placed the throne of their king at this location.[133] The king is the conduit for sacred energy into worldly energy. It is as if God's power must travel through one's being first through the head, down through the spine and through the heart to the earth. And the king is the route of this sacred energy.

In the film, *First Knight,* King Arthur instructs Lancelot, who is to become the ideal warrior once knighted. Arthur's words are those of an archetypal king:

> "Now, I know the truth" [says Arthur]. "You care nothing for yourself…no wealth, no home, just the passionate spirit that drives you on. God uses people like you, Lancelot, because your heart is open."

The king energy in Arthur assures him that Lancelot is potentially an expression of God because his "heart is open." Arthur's view of the world, his kingdom and his subjects is reflected in this conversation with Lancelot:

> "I believe that every life is precious, even the life of strangers. If you must die, die serving something greater than yourself."

Here, Arthur displays his celebration of life and then teaches Lancelot the meaning of commitment. He continues,

> "Better still, live and serve."
>
> "The roundtable!" [says Lancelot].
>
> "Yes, no head, no foot, everyone equal. Even the king" [says Arthur].

Arthur experiences inner order and hungers to affirm others, not have power over them. He is the caretaker of his subjects.

> "Lancelot, just a thought. A man who fears nothing is a man who loves nothing. If you love nothing, what joy is there in your life?"

The king's most prominent emotional expression is joy—joy with life. The shadow side of the king, the expression of immature masculinity includes the aspects on the right below:

KING

Bright Energy	Shadow Energy
Leader	Tyrant
Protector	Exploiter
Transfuse sacred energy	Impotent
Celebrates life	Fears new life
Centered	Destructive
Generative	Controlling
Ordered	Patriarchal
Blesses	Degrades others

Lover

In contrast to the father energy of the king, lover energy facilitates more companionship. The Lover is the expression of personal concern regardless of the collective demands of the people of the kingdom. The lover "goes his own way, seeks individual relationships and his own individuality."[134] In myth the lover is represented by Tolkien's Sam Gamgee, by Peter Pan and Adonis...all eternal seekers. The lover's orientation is to love in any form, and he lacks boundaries in the search. The expression of lover energy is found in the Roman *amour* or, the Hindu *tantra*, the complete union of one body and soul with another. But, it is also found in *agape*, what the Bible calls "brotherly love." Lover energy includes erotic love for the sake of stimulus alone.

The Lover is also the energy of spirituality. With no boundary to his search for feeling, emotion and stimulus, in sex, food and other hungers, the lover is our source of insight into the interconnectedness of all life. He cannot but be joined with all others. This is his spiritual message. "The Lover is the archetype of play and of 'display', of healthy embodiment, of being in the world of sensuous pleasure and in one's own body *without shame*."[135] This is the archetype of both libido and of

Eros. Eros is Freud's "life instinct" and the energy that fuels the life instinct, the libido. Plato said Eros was the yearning of the soul for union with the divine.

In the film, *The Fisher King,* Robin Williams plays the part of a teacher driven to apparent mental illness after the death of his wife. He depicts a man free of inhibition, without social graces, who can describe the source of his sensations. Williams is one of the most playful and fun-focused actors in Hollywood. But he is also a recovering drug addict. Addiction is one of the shadow sides of the lover—he often doesn't resist compulsive use of drugs. In his personal life, Williams struggles with his shadow as well. Once addicted, a person is always vulnerable to the use of drugs.

At one point in the film, Williams's character is in the park with his alcoholic friend, Jack, who is constantly caught off guard by Williams's child-like behavior.

> "I'm cloud busting Jack. Ever tried it?" [Williams says as he strips naked in a public place]. "You concentrate in the clouds, lay on your back and you break them apart with your mind" [he continues]. "You have to be nude, Jack. You have to build psychic energy."
>
> "You can't do this. This is New York!" [says Jack]. "No one is allowed to be nude in a park in New York! It is too midwestern."
>
> "Come on, Jack. It's wild. It is freeing" [says Williams, dancing about nude in the moonlight].
>
> "The air on your body. The nipples are hard. Your little guy dangling in the wind."
>
> "Hey, hey. Come on" [begs Jack].

But Williams's character insists on running about and rolling in the grass naked.

To gain access to the energy of this archetype, men must experience the emotion of *grief.* The route to the king's energy is joy but to be in your lover, one must let go and allow the welling up of emotion that is trapped by unresolved sorrow.

The shadow side of the lover is, once again, listed on the right side:

LOVER

Bright Energy	Shadow Energy
Playful	Restless
Intuitive	Disrespects other people's Boundaries
Spiritual	Lacks boundaries
Sensuous	Addicted
Connection through feeling	Lacks enthusiasm

Poet Kahlil Gibran reminds us concerning the lover and his shadow side:

When love beckons to you, follow him,
Though his ways are hard and steep.
And when his wings enfold you yield to him.
Though the sword hidden among his
Pinions may wound you.
And when he speaks to you believe in him,
Though his voice may shatter your
Dreams as the north wind lays waste the garden.[136]

Warrior

The warrior's energy is outgoing, assertive and aggressive. When making choices like "fight or flight," his response is to attack or, at minimum, to stand his ground and defend the boundaries. His reference is the collective values of his community, his state or country. His energy is devoted to maintaining high principles and he has a commitment to beliefs higher than himself. This archetype is a "go-getter." He fights, strives and accomplishes on behalf of the community, the state or the ruler he admires. He is not interested in ruling or in being receptive or wise. He is concerned with focusing personal will and is proud of his prowess in this effort.

Examples of the warrior in myth are Achilles and Lancelot. Real life warriors include Joan of Arc, the heroes of the Alamo and the samurai defenders of the Shogun.

In myth we often run across a *hero*. This archetype comes close to warrior status but lacks maturity. The hero is a stage of boyhood development. The hero likes to impress others, while the warrior cares nothing for how he is regarded, but rather needs to reach his goal. What the hero does is energize the boy to enable him to break with the mother and father at the end of boyhood and face the difficult task of growing up.

To be willing to self-annihilate in the accomplishment of a goal leaves the warrior with an emotional distance from other people. He can't make his strategic decisions if he allows passion or emotion to cloud his thinking. In this way, he is somewhat like the intellectual magician archetype. He is so detached in his strategy that he is able to accept his imminent death. He is energized by the knowledge that life is short.

The warrior is enthusiastic about strength, skill, power and accuracy. He employs spiritual, psychological and physical prowess to win. He is "cool" in that he only uses as much energy as is needed for the task. He doesn't need to impress others with his mastery of the technology that helped him get to his goal. His confidence and commitment brings about an unbreakable spirit of will. Skill and discipline combined with confidence causes others to have trust in his ability and it energizes others.

In the film, *The American President,* Michael Douglas portrays the chief executive. In one scene, he must respond to an attack by Libya. A counterattack could quell the enemy, but it would also cause the death of many innocent Libyan citizens. He has just asked his advisors what else will be hit in Tripoli if the United States bombs its target.

"Nothing, unless we miss" [answers a general].

"Are we going to miss?" [asks the President].

"No, sir" [the general says].

"And how many people are working in the building we are bombing?" [the President inquires nervously].

"We've been all through this" [a military advisor states in a frustrated voice].

"How many people are working in the damn building?" [the President responds angrily].

"I have the numbers here, Mr. President" [reports an associate].

"What shift has the fewest people, the night shift right?" [retorts the President].

"By far, sir" [the associate says].

"What time does the night shift start?" [asks the President].

"They are on right now, sir" [responds the associate].

The President stares into space for a moment, takes a deep breath. A general says to him,

"Mr. President?"

"Attack" [responds the President].

The warrior experiences emotion as a consequence of his decisions but those decisions are reached in a calculated and careful manner. The emotion that brings one into the warrior's energy is *anger*. Anger doesn't characterize warrior energy but one must "go into their anger" to find the warrior in themselves.

The shadow side of the warrior is contrasted with the bright side below:

WARRIOR

Bright Energy	*Shadow Energy*
Assertive	Passive-aggressive
Committed to transpersonal goal	Cowardly
Emotionally detached	Cruel
Strategist	Hates weakness
Knows his limitations	Sadist
Establishes firm boundaries	Masochist

Magician

This archetype is the master of knowledge. He is idea-oriented rather than person-oriented. He listens, receives, and perceives. He is a scholar, teacher, seer and philosopher. The magician lives in the expression of a man's unconscious. There is something eerie about the magician as if he has access to knowledge denied to most of us. This archetype is, therefore, felt to be magical or mystical. He can be a source of inspiration or of confusion. This archetype mediates the power of the psyche more than the other three masculine archetypes. In history, Socrates and Moses are good examples, and in myth one finds magicians like Ben (Obi-Wan) Kenobi of *Star Wars* and Camelot's Merlin. A magician is one who seemingly has supernatural powers. Mystics, doctors, counselors and ministers seemingly have supernatural powers, or at least, their confidence in doing what others find baffling can give that impression.

Some believe that "in order to find our own individual centers, we need to be able to access the inner Magician."[137] The magician's wisdom and expertise guide us in our understanding of self. So, even though this archetype is really in his head, we need his focus on the intellectual to grasp the meaning of life. Mature masculinity depends on the balance of the fourfold way: intellectual; psychological; spiritual; and physical. In many cultures the magician is the energy behind the "ritual elder" who facilitates initiation ceremonies such as marriage, the ordaining of priests and other rites of passage.

It is from the magician archetype that we are moved to thoughtfulness, reflection and insight. Whereas the lover acts on intuition and feeling, the magician reads the world like a mathematician, a scientist. He is unemotional. He watches life rather than lives it. Through this emotional separation the magician protects us from the boundless love of the lover, the sometimes naive joy of the king and the anger of the warrior.

In the first *Star Wars* film, Jedi knight and magician, Ben (Obi-Wan) Kenobi, advises Luke Skywalker on the role of the force in the life of a space age warrior:

"Remember Luke, a Jedi can feel the force flowing through him" [says Ben].

"You mean it controls your actions?" [asks Skywalker as he tries out his light sabre].

"Partially, but it also obeys your commands" [responds Ben].

Skywalker tries with frustration to utilize the force but can't quite grasp it. Ben offers him a helmet that block's Luke's vision.

"This time, let go your conscious self, and act on insight" [the magician asserts with utter confidence in the force, the universal power Ben understands well].

"I can't even see. How am I supposed to fight?" [asks Skywalker].

"Your eyes can deceive you. Don't trust them" [Ben suggests]. "Stretch out with your feelings."

To access magician energy, a man must face his fear. The magician taps the unknown, the unconscious and the universe. These are sources of frightening power. The shadow of the magician has been repressed for the sake of a mature expression of masculinity. His two sides include:

MAGICIAN

Bright Energy	Shadow Energy
Master of knowledge	Calls forth the demonic
Healer	Manipulator
Insight	Illusive
Protection from emotional irrationality	Stands too far back from real life
Scientist, mathematician	Dishonest
Shaman	Trickster

The KLWM archetypes are a rich source of reference when asking, "What is a grown-up man?" We began, however, with a discussion of the three basic male role prescriptions: protector; provider; teacher. Further, our task is to integrate both the archetypes and the roles into modern life. Finally, we can demonstrate that an elder is a model of mature masculinity when he exhibits a balanced and modern expression of these archetypes and roles.

You can find the four masculine archetypes in each of the three roles. The *protector* is a king in his stewardship of people and the earth. He is a lover as he experiences passion for being with his family and strives to keep it together by working hand-in-hand with his wife. He is a warrior when he stands up for ideals and standards that make his children safer as they grow and experience adulthood. He is a magician when he articulates the rights of men, women and children.

The *provider* is kingly as he finds the source of his personal power and does not seek power for its own sake. He is lover-like as he seeks his passion in life and follows it. Passion is far more important to the lover in us than is wealth or things we accumulate. The provider utilizes warrior energy as he cares for his health, both physical and psychological. The warrior knows he must be fit to tackle the job of living a long life. The provider utilizes magician energy as he joins with his wife to assess who is best suited to care for the home with gender being a minor part of the equation.

The *teacher* role and the magician archetype are very similar. In the traditional cultures of pre-modern times the men found themselves "on the perimeter" of the community. They were defending the village but also assessing the nature of the world that lay beyond the edge of the community. A man today can bring home a description of the world beyond the home. He can teach about law, politics, culture and earning a living. He teaches about religion with masculine energy.

The Masculine and the Feminine

Finally, as we gear up for a twenty-first century expression of masculinity, we must address femininity as well. This is a dual process requiring the expression of the feminine energy in ourselves and in an interplay with women. One will recall that the feminine energy in men's psyche is called the *anima*. This is the unconscious feminine side of men. In women, the unconscious masculine energy comes from their *animus*.

When a man experiences a passionate attraction to a specific woman, it is because she seems to embody his *anima*.

Over the past few generations, men and women have changed their expression both of gender and of energy. For example, women have made a gender shift toward birthing out of wedlock. The numbers are increasing annually. This requires a single parent female to tap her animus more often. To model for her children a passion for achievement, for example, she needs masculine energy. To model an appreciation for beauty in nature, on the other hand, she can spontaneously act female, for this is more natural to a woman than a man. A spontaneous, natural expression of masculinity is problem-solving. It has benefited modern men in tackling the problem of harassment, for example. In the latter part of this century, men have increasingly tried to address their inclination to harass females in the workplace. To be more loving, respectful and anxious to relate to women as equals rather than sexual objects, they have drawn upon their anima.

The men who will move about in the twenty-first century with the most ease are those who accept the changes that have occurred in men and women in this century. At the same time, honoring the archetypal feminine is needed just as much as the masculine. Relating to women is another dual process: addressing both the woman and her archetypal feminine energy. Therefore, let's review masculine and contrast it to what the experts call *feminine*, keeping in mind these are behaviors, not genders.

MASCULINE	FEMININE
Values power, competency, efficiency and achievement	Values loving, communicating, beauty, and relating
Needs to learn to listen to female more	Gives unsolicited advice
Needs to leave it alone if it is working	Nurturing and intuitive
Enjoys out-of-doors, news weather and sports	Enjoys personal growth.
Keeps problems to himself	Wants to talk it out

MASCULINE	FEMININE
Views talking as competition, a negotiation of status and preserving one's independence	Views talking as relaxing, connecting
Offers solutions	Wants to be heard.
Has political, economic, military and physical power	Has emotional, moral and sexual power
Fears giving	Fears receiving
Challenged by and conquers in the sexual arena	Sees sex as part of a love relationship
Communicates literally	Communicates figuratively
	Is spirituality oriented in early life

The New Male Elder

Today's elder is one who respects the "new male" expression of masculinity. The new male is a man who believes he is hard-wired in his expression of *historical maleness* but who has a feel for the most effective and healthy expression of modern maleness, mature masculinity. A twenty-first century expression of masculinity requires an adaptation to the changes in gender expression that were wrought by the social revolutions of the 1960s, the introspection of the 1970s, the self-indulgence of the 1980s and the millennial threshold of the 1990s.

Elderhood of the twenty-first century is an expression of New Maleness. This modern manifestation of maturity is built on a modernization of the three male roles. It requires a balanced expression of masculine and feminine energy.

The task of the new male elder is to integrate as much of the five processes discussed above into his expression of self. The five processes again are:

1. Expressing the energy of each archetype in a balanced way against the other three

2. Keeping our shadow in check and not feeling too much guilt about having a dark side

3. Passing through adolescence and building upon the boyhood archetypes to allow the expression of the "mature" masculine archetypes

4. Playing the roles of protector, provider and teacher in a way that matches the needs of the twenty-first century

5. Expressing both the masculine and feminine energies from within ourselves and projecting our anima onto some very special other who embodies our underdeveloped feminine

❖   ❖   ❖   ❖

Father Bert, An elder with over sixty-five years life experience

Mentoring is a community experience passing on the wisdom of the community, to members of the community authenticated by the community itself.

Bert was one of the finest examples of the magician, a "crusty old elder." He was outspoken and could be cheeky when impassioned about an issue. He didn't kid himself, however, about the role of older men in the community. Bert was a sixty-seven-year-old Catholic priest that has devoted his career to community development on behalf of the needy. Before his death in 2000, he told me that elders must receive community validation before they can be useful. He said, "In America we prize individual autonomy but bemoan the absence of elders." Elders who live without the endorsement of those they serve are not credible. Bert said he passes on wisdom that he gained from the faith and experience of the wider community, members of the congregation, fellow elders and friends. "Hence mentoring is also a community experience passing on the wisdom of the community, to members of the community, authenticated by the community itself," he said.

I met Bert many years ago when I was seeking an annulment of my first marriage. The Catholic Church, of which my new wife was a member, believed that my first marriage should be annulled before the second one could be sanctified. When I sought Bert's advice on the process, he asked me if my first marriage was a loving one even though it was short and occurred when I was very immature. I told him that it was based on love. He said that the church sometimes gets caught up in its rules and forgets that the basis for all the laws is love, which is the same thing as God. A loving way to remember my first wife, he said, would be to hold precious the memory of the good parts of the marriage and not annul it.

Bert was a man of spirit first and a defender of church doctrine second. He sensed how bureaucratic I found the process of annulment to be and became an advocate for me in spirit. He agreed that my former wife and I had tried to make a go of a commitment but that the failure of the marriage was only evidence of our immaturity. He asked if my present wife would understand if I withdrew my application for an annulment. She would, I told him, and I left his presence with his loving encouragement to follow my heart. I dropped the idea of annulling my first marriage and have never regretted it.

Chapter V

BECOMING AN ELDER

To become wise I need only live,
To be trusted as wise,
Oh, for any man to give,
And have the gift be taken with celebration,
Must come first the blessings:
One from the elder's heart and one from posterity

The process of becoming an elder requires that a man seek the expression of eldership. How can a man access his elder energy and express eldership? There are three processes that encourage growth into eldership, and we will review each in this chapter.

The first is to recognize and embrace the fact that eldership is a *stage of development*. The second is *initiation* into eldership. The third and most complex is to do the intellectual, psychological and spiritual personal work necessary to grow into eldership. The man who expresses eldership is doing something for himself and his community. He is sharing his knowledge and skill in the second half of life. And he is learning in a way only possible through the give-and-take of the mentoring relationship.

The man who expresses eldership maintains a connection to those who would gain from his elderhood. He is interesting, energizing and passionate. These qualities inspire young people who become drawn to him. The process is to first find your elder energy, then be recognized by the young as an elder and finally, to do the work necessary to grow up and act like an elder.

Eldership As a Stage of Personal Growth

Poets, psychologists and anthropologists have all recognized that there are predictable stages of human development that include eldership. They call it different names, but in poetry, psychology and social anthropology, stages of personal growth can be found that include a generative, spiritual maturity in the second half of life. I call this stage *eldership.* Let's consider four models of personal growth that suggest strongly that eldership happens naturally if allowed to become a part of your growth into mature masculinity.

Erikson

Erik Erikson, M.D., asserted in 1950 that there are eight steps in adapting psychologically and socially to life. There are other psychologists and educators who suggest that we can identify stages of *cognitive* and *moral* development as well. Research done since 1950 has shown that adult life does not necessarily progress through fixed, predictable steps. Erikson's work provides, however, a perspective that has earned common acceptance. Many psychologists have divided human development into eight stages of life because of Erikson's work. Each stage is characterized by a "crisis" that must be resolved for healthy development to occur. Each developmental task that stirs eldership in a man is in *italics*.

ERIKSON'S STAGES

1. First year of life   Crisis: Trust versus Mistrust

2. Toddler   Crisis: Autonomy vs. Shame and Guilt

3. Preschooler   Crisis: Initiative vs. Guilt

4. School age   Crisis: Competence vs. Inferiority

5. Adolescence   Crisis: Identity vs. Role Confusion

6. Young adulthood   Crisis: Intimacy vs. Isolation

7. Adulthood   Crisis: *Generativity* vs. Stagnation

8. Maturity   Crisis: *Ego Integrity* vs. Despair

Stage theories like Erikson's suggest that there are "passages" people must traverse in life. As we review a few of the stage theories, keep in mind that development is never finished nor easily put into a formula. The "crisis" of one stage may reawaken during another stage. Identity crises, for example, are not only present in adolescence. The development of competence is a dynamic process that occurs throughout life and not just in Erikson's fourth stage. Children develop because of biological changes dictated by genetics as well as psychosocial forces. However, environmental and social forces have more impact on adult development.

More important than the specific stages within a theory are the general challenges we face as we mature. Erikson believed these challenges included at least *affiliation, generativity and ego integrity.* "Ego integrity…implies an emotional integration which permits participation by followership as well as acceptance of the responsibility of leadership."[138] He took the word "generative," which means the power to generate, and popularized it as the noun "generativity." He said that his stages consisted mostly of youth, but had his theory been focused on adulthood, "generativity" would have been his central issue. Generativity is the quality that makes men into teachers and creative and learning creatures.

Recreation, Depletion, Retirement

The American attitude about the second half of life leads to an occupation with *recreation, depletion and retirement.* This view focuses mostly on retreating, not generating! In our move to "retire," we pull away from younger people and our opportunity for "affiliation" diminishes. "Ego integrity" facilitates the acceptance of one's mortality. Depletion is only an aspect of mortality, not a condition you need to fear. The crisis for mature adults is to avoid despair about depletion. The despair leads to the belief that life is too short to start another life consisting of mentoring, teaching and sharing the wisdom gained from long life experience.

There is a challenge implicit in Erikson's last two stages of life. In middle age (between forty and fifty-five years), we can play, attempt to stem the pace of depletion and retreat from life's challenges. But we can also be generative! Generativity is a concern for supporting and guiding the next generation. What nourishes the soul in the second half of life? Travel, golf, fishing, a new business venture, or painting do it for some. However, they must accept responsibility for not having shared their wisdom if these activities cause them to avoid contact with the younger generation. To become a resource to others, we must be accessible. Traditional second-half-of-life activities make us inaccessible. How do those who would receive our legacy find us? How confident are we that we have wisdom?

In the final stage of life, older adults can either consider life meaningful or despair about goals not reached. To accomplish ego integrity, older people must accomplish all of the following:

- develop trust, autonomy and independence
- show initiative
- remain industrious
- have a definable identity
- seek affiliation
- accept their mortality
- seed the young with good ideas

The growth we attained in the prior stages gives us confidence that we have learned something valuable in living a long life. Eldership is a display of passion, skill and knowledge that energizes others while nurturing the soul of the elder. In chapter two we considered the devastating impact of industrialization, immigration and war on men's souls and how they led to an "impoverishment" of men. Impoverishment is the opposite of fertility and generativity. Men lost touch with the land, with the family and, therefore, lost touch with the catalysts to growth into maturity. Human beings need the ability to confront, struggle with and advance through stages of growth—the "passages."

Bly

In poet Robert Bly's controversial book, *Iron John,* the author addresses the effect of losing touch with our roots and the family traditions that facilitate growth. Bly resurrects a fairy tale in which a mentor guides a young man through eight stages of growth unique to men. Being off the land and in the city seeking wealth, men in the nineteenth century began to lose touch with their mentors. These mentors were primarily the fathers and grandfathers the factory workers had left behind on family farms. Bly mourns the impoverishment that resulted from losing contact with our fathers, both geographically and emotionally. He hungers for male initiation rites more common in the pre-industrial world. Bly's eight stages have been depicted often in myths throughout history. It is interesting that all the stage theorists reviewed here count seven or eight stages of growth whether they have studied poetry, myth, psychology, anthropology or the customs of indigenous cultures.

BLY'S STAGES
(Eldership in *italics*)

1. Early childhood   Task: Bonding with Mother
2. Late childhood   Task: Leaving the Mother
3. Early adolescence   Task: Bonding with Father
4. Late adolescence   Task: Leaving the Father
5. Early adulthood   Task: The Quest
6. Young adulthood   Task: *Working with the Mentor*
7. Adulthood   Task: *Apprenticeship*
8. Maturity   Task: *Integration of the Masculine and the Feminine*

Bly is concerned primarily with the development of gender identity and learning about the expression of masculine and feminine energy. We are born of the mother and nourished by her feminine passion for nourishing, enfolding and shielding the child. The study of maternal-infant bonding has shown that when a child and his mother bond physically and psychologically, the child's future is more likely to include blessings such as good health, high IQ and good social skills. The challenge in early childhood is to connect with the nurturing power of our feminine parent. Erikson would call this a major "trust" experience.

Next, a boy must leave the overwhelming influence of the mother and seek balance in the power of the masculine. In Bly's story, the mother keeps the key to the masculine. To access the power of the masculine, a child needs to come to his father through his mother, leaving her and taking the key to the cage that houses Iron John, the masculine aspect of a boy's soul. The challenge in the second stage of both Erikson's and Bly's models is to risk autonomy and bond with the father who models initiative in contrast to the sheltering of the mother.

The increasing problems of fatherlessness and out-of-wedlock births deprive young boys and girls of the opportunity to experience a male model. If our fathers cannot give us what we need to access the masculine in ourselves, we can get stuck in immature masculinity. An answer to this dilemma is male eldership. In ancient times the older men would teach the younger men how to become healthy men. In today's world, mature older men could fill this role if they were accessible. In Bly's model, the developing male must eventually leave the sphere of the father as well as the mother. If an older mature man cannot play the role of father in a boy's life, he can at least assist the boy's development by playing a role in the *apprenticeship.* Mentors are essential to the developing man's growth into self-identity and competence as "his own man." An apprentice is a learner. Like Levinson's mentor referred to in chapter one, the ideal advocate or model for the apprentice is not a father but rather a more objective older male who could, someday, even become a peer. This is an excellent opportunity for the man wanting to express eldership. In Pat Conroy's novel, *Beach Music,* we find this description of one boy's mentor:

> Jordan turned his blue eyes at the drawling, overweight coach who ran a gas station for a living and brought an irrepressible love of sport and young boys to the task of coaching…. Jordan saw the goodness of the man below the primitive, fascist exterior that is the general rule among the southern fraternity of coaches. It was the man's basic and abiding sweetness that Jordan felt as coach Langford put the ball back into Jordan's glove and said, "Son, now I'd like to see you strike him out."

In Erikson's model, completing the development of a mature self requires an experience of intimacy, generativity, and finally, balance (what he calls "ego integrity"). Bly would have us reach these goals through a complete enfolding of both the masculine and feminine energy in our psyche. Intimacy and generativity are feminine qualities, but men express them differently than women. These qualities are energizing when expressed by men. They are a source of peace and serenity when expressed by women. The integration of feminine and masculine happens in maturity.

The man in *Iron John* was about fifty years old when he reached the last developmental stage. "Some flower has finally unfolded and blossomed…the young man has received…a grounding that allows him to reconnect with some creativity [i.e., something feminine] that would have frightened him when he was younger…eventually, at fifty or fifty-five, we feel a golden ring on the finger again."[139] The challenge to men in the second half of life is to become an advocate for a young man's development, but especially at the time the young man is in Bly's sixth and seventh stages: the arrival of the mentor and the apprenticeship. Mature masculinity, the basis of true eldership, is possible only after having reached a point where the elder is able to express a balance of both masculine and feminine energy. He must then utilize this balance of energy as a model for the next generation.

Arrien

Anthropologist Angeles Arrien also believes there are eight stages of development. She finds her model in her review of cultures throughout the world. She mixes in some myth and comes up with eight "gates" through which we must pass if we are to fully mature.

ARRIEN'S STAGES
(Eldership in *italics*)

<u>Youth</u>

1. The silver gate	Challenge: birth and all that is new.
2. The white picket fence	Challenge: taking a look at the roles we play.
3. The clay gate	Challenge: looking into the mystery of sensuality and sexuality.

Middle Age

4. The black and white gate   Challenge: facing our fear and pride.

5. The rustic gate   Challenge: reviewing our creativity and assessing whether it aligns with our life calling and passions.

Maturity

6. The bone gate   Challenge: *reclamation of the authentic self so as to* allow modeling of character and integrity.

7. The natural gate   Challenge: *reviewing the content ment of our past life* and what brings contentment now.

8. The gold gate   Challenge: *letting go of attach ments and embodying* spiritual work which includes managing fear.

Arrien's description of the stages of life is almost too abstruse. She does offer, however, another view of the challenge of eldership. She teaches that the goal of the first part of life is to "seek success" and that this requires exploring our strengths and talents. The challenge of the first two gates and the white picket fence passage is in this exploration. In the middle of life she believes we transform and begin to reclaim our authentic selves—selves that were confused and masked by our exploration of roles and opportunities for success and our response to social expectations.

Her study of multiple culture leads the anthropologist to suggest that the challenge of late life is to develop your character. Also, she asserts this requires being generative and experiencing transcendence facilitated by compassion and wisdom. This character development leads to mentoring, coaching and stewardship of people in the middle of life. In Arrien's model, the first elder quality is the challenge at the bone gate— reclamation of the authentic self to allow modeling of character and integrity. An example of this type of modeling is living the life of the *blessing way.* Arrien states that this entails, in part, committing daily to setting sacred intention through prayer or some type of visible ceremony. The ritual also includes giving gratitude and making a life affirming action at least once daily.[140]

Moore and Gillette

When, in chapter three, we reviewed the four masculine powers or archetypes of King, Lover, Warrior and Magician, much of what I shared came from the work of Robert Moore, a psychoanalyst, and his co-author, Douglas Gillette, a mythologist and counselor. These men found a consistent pattern throughout world cultures in male growth and development. They refer to their seven stages as *stages of initiation.* They found that masculine initiation in most cultures was a process with numerous steps. These two men assert that the same seven stages are traversed when accessing any of the four masculine powers.

MOORE AND GILLETTE'S STAGES
(Eldership in *italics*)

Youth

First stage of initiation	Challenge: a man becomes a Quester for something he lacks but senses it as his mission.
Second stage of initiation	Challenge: locating the qualities in himself he longs to have, he begins by seeing them only in other persons, objects and institutions.
Third stage of initiation	Challenge: experiencing the power of King, Lover, Warrior, and/or Magician energy in oneself.

Middle life

Fourth stage | Challenge: where at first the man only had a slight grasp of his mission and then almost being possessed by it, here he realizes the work necessary to develop into maturity.

Maturity,

Fifth stage | Challenge: mastering of the power (i.e. King, Lover, Warrior or Magician)

Sixth stage of initiation | Challenge: *steward one's powers for the sake of others* thus bringing our capacities into service.

The last stage is the most important for elders. It is here, in maturity, that you move from "possession" of skill and wisdom to "use" of these resources for the sake of man and the earth. There are millions of competent men who have reached fifth-degree initiations who are competent but they "have not yet begun to see that their remaining and most critical challenge is one of stewardship for the community of Earth."[141] Being grown up means that you utilize your wisdom for the sake of others. Our North American focus on second-half-of-life recreation, depletion and retirement limits us to a fifth-degree initiation at best.

The first of three ways to move yourself into elder status, then, is to decide whether being elder-like is necessary to complete human development. The people quoted above believe it to be essential. Erikson told us that adulthood is defined in part as facing the crisis of generativity versus the despair of believing you have nothing to offer. Erikson's final crisis is to avoid despair about our mortality through a four-fold balance he calls "ego integrity." The *Fourfold way* is intellectual, emotional, spiritual and physical. The poet, Robert Bly, takes us in a different direction.

Bly asserts that growing up requires an apprenticeship to adulthood. After completing the training satisfactorily in the apprenticeship, you let go of many of the tools of growing up. You become self-actualized, fulfilling your potentials and setting your own standards. Bly says that we accomplish this through a balanced expression of both masculine and feminine energy. This is another way of reaching Erikson's "ego integrity." Arrien says that one goal in maturity is to let go of attachments and social expectations and incorporate your spiritual work. You could call this "following your heart." She lays out the challenge that older people are "responsible" for modeling integrity and good character. Elders would agree with her. Moore and Gillette, then, put development into the framework of *initiations*. Initiation is the capacity to learn something new and demonstrate it to someone else. The final challenge in their seventh stage of initiation is for us to steward our power, our wisdom, for the sake of others. He adds to the other three-stage theories the step where you demonstrate for others that you have been initiated into adulthood.

Is it possible to reach full maturity and avoid the expression of eldership? Yes. You can live a rich life, have fun and model many adult attributes without becoming an elder, but an elder is the best example of a mature and balanced man. Why concern yourself with becoming an elder, though, when you feel you have already contributed a lot as a parent, a spouse, a citizen and a worker? Both the elder and the community must experience the energy of eldership before either can have the peak experience of being fully alive, flourish and thrive. All adults are sixth-level initiates, but the elder has balanced in a fourfold way, has reclaimed his authentic self and has become a model of good character and ego integrity. Now that you can envision becoming an elder, let's look at the second process that brings about elder behavior in older men—*initiation*.

The Initiation of an Elder

Unlike the young man, the elder's journey into adulthood is not one of becoming a unique psychological individual. The elder moves toward being initiated into a journey of partnership and community.

This shift occurs in midlife and is so important that it usually disrupts his peace. Common are persistent feelings of:

- Boredom
- Disillusionment with life
- Disappearance of the Dream we create in our youth
- Bouts of depression filled with regret
- Heightened sense of your mortality and life's limited duration

There is a need for a ritual, ceremony or initiation that facilitates the transition called *midlife,* as well as eldership.

In chapter one, we reviewed briefly the idea of initiation and rites of passage. These rituals function to move individuals through transition periods in their lives. They have the effect of making the transition transformative. They give transitions personal and cultural significance. In the West, we have *practices* that are common to transitions, like a father presenting his son with a shotgun at a time the father felt his son was moving out of childhood into adolescence. These practices are common to our experience and imply that we are in the midst of transitions, but they lack the solemnity of the rituals for which I hunger. For example, many cultures have initiation ceremonies for children who have become capable of sexual reproduction. To some, the word "initiation" means "puberty rites by virtue of which adolescents gain access to the sacred, to knowledge, and to sexuality by which, in short, they become human beings."[142] However, a person can also be initiated into a fraternity, a marriage or priesthood. We have learned much about initiation from the puberty rites of various cultures, but there are many life transitions that rituals can facilitate.

The preparation and the testing of the initiates in most rites of passage are the responsibility of the elders. The supervision of initiations by older people is needed but it makes sense only if these people have been initiated themselves or, through some other process, have taken ownership of their eldership. Western man has a grasp of some of the psychological functions of rites of passage, but this is the extent of elder knowledge of transitions in most cultures of the New World. We looked above at the four aspects of transition as the West views and values them: shock; resistance; exploration; adaptation. Parents, grandparents and other mentors must understand that the process of change has these four challenges, but there is a "mystery" about growth and development that we need to respect as well.

Sacred Eldership

My emulation of the initiations performed in indigenous cultures is charged by my belief that we need to integrate the sacred mystery with the psychological and social purposes of celebrating an individual's life transitions. We can find a microcosm of our more complex secular civilization in small, more primitive societies, past and present. What we call *primitive* is what we once were! As society progresses, the people believe that they become different and more advanced than their predecessors. In primitive cultures man is more spiritual, almost unable to separate the sacred from the secular. Aspects of the holy enter most phases of life. Being born, reaching puberty and even visiting another culture are all acts that fall within the sacred sphere among indigenous people. These are transitions, and all transitions mean that a form of birth and death are experienced. The "shock" and "resistance" we respect in the West are reactions to both a new challenge (i.e. a birth) and the close of something familiar (i.e. death).

Modern, *advanced* cultures have lost confidence in many sacred practices like prayer, affirmation and rites of passage. To us they seem speculative, amorphous and a waste of time. As cultures *progress*, "change" becomes a constant, the pace picks up and time management becomes essential. In "managing time" and "coping with change"—hallmarks of the modern stress manager—we are inclined to discard the least concrete and least useful from our behavior. We believe that sacred practices only work if we have faith in them. However, "as we move downward on the scale of civilizations...we cannot fail to note an ever increasing domination of the secular by the sacred."[143] In the world of primitive people, a man can't pass from the secular to the sacred without going through some kind of ritual.

In the secular world of the West, a man passes from midlife into the second half of life by intellectual and economic means. Our churches have the word "elder" in their parlance, but today, even religion gives much less meaning to the role than did the sacred institutions of ancient times. We identify those who have passed into the second half of life by looking to secular institutions such as the Social Security Administration, the workplace, and the American Association of Retired Persons. These organizations define when we are "old enough" or "too old." Each of these groups honors our old age economically through stipends and price breaks. These institutions have the effect of moving us into adulthood. However, an initiation ritual could attribute a divinely sanctioned meaning to a man's passage into old age. Ritual places a man within the context of the culture's myths and traditions, giving him recognition and confirmation that a transition has occurred.

Remember that our fear of aging has contributed to our fear of old people. Unlike the behavior in traditional cultures, the mode today is to dismiss the traditions as suffocating, slow and unproductive. In pre-industrial times, the elders utilizing ritual to imprint our brains passed on values and attitudes without many questions from generation to generation. We have more confidence today in the resilient young than the wise old. Our emphasis is on rebellion against the traditions of the fathers and solidarity within our peer group. With the influence of modern, initiated elders the young could develop trust. The modern elder can't establish credibility only from tradition or from unquestioned conformity to peer group pressure.

Phases of Initiation

With an eye toward facilitating the development of mature men, then, I will define the elements of an initiation ceremony that honors the elder "rite of passage." Rites of passage, from the early Christian rituals to those of indigenous cultures to the process of incorporating a recruit into the modern military, have three phases. Let's review these phases in order: *separation, threshold and incorporation.*

Separation comprises behaviors that suggest the detachment of a person from an old set of cultural conditions. All transitions have both losses and gains. Something ends while, at the same time, new opportunities present themselves. The separation phase of rites is like a small death. It is the first of the three phases. In indigenous cultures, initiates are sometimes buried or required to lie motionless during the separation phase of a rite. Some initiates are forced to live for a time with masked men who symbolize the dead. Military recruits sacrifice their civilian persona as their mother's son, accept a number and a uniform and then face the dreaded military haircut. Cutting hair is common to many ancient rites of passage. This act connotes a dedication of a part of yourself to the new condition of life you enter while relinquishing the part you leave behind.

During the next phase, the state of mind of the initiate and his status in his community is uncertain. This is common to all of us when we pass through important life transitions. We lose balance and drift between the "devil and the deep blue sea." This *threshold* phase is like land that has been plowed but not yet seeded. The initiate encounters his limits and steps formally into the unknown. This requires training and mentoring because the initiate is lost, homeless and usually confused. In some fraternal organizations, this is the time of instruction that precedes confirmation as a member. The instruction is usually secret and imparts knowledge allowed only among initiates who are passing through the threshold phase. Those cultures and institutions that have utilized rites of passage for centuries believe the new knowledge imprints the initiate, as a seal impresses wax, with the characteristics of a new state of being.

In the *incorporation* phase, the initiate is enfolded by a community that recognizes him as a new member whose initiation is complete. Among the Zuni of New Mexico, men wearing masks during the threshold phase remove their masks during incorporation, the last part of the initiation ritual. By this act they show the initiate that they really are men, not gods as they pretended earlier, and want him to join them as an equal.[144] In the military, the recruit is awarded his stripes as symbols of his incorporation into the ranks of fully trained soldiers. In this third phase, the initiate's passage is consummated. He is stable once again and, therefore, has rights and obligations to the community and is expected to follow customs and ascribe to delineated ethical standards.

The Process: Introduction

The man who would be an initiate in this honoring of eldership can expect the full process to take no less than six months. However, the decision about when the ritual reaches the threshold and incorporation phases belongs to the elder initiate. When the initiate feels he is ready to accept of the mantle of eldership, the initiation begins. It begins with the initiate's decision to participate in the rite and ends with a ceremony. The initiate alone can manage the rite, but I recommend assigning the role of *ritual elder* to another man who is in the second half of life whom the initiate trusts. Because we have not honored elders in this culture for so many generations, you may have a hard time identifying people you feel express elder energy. Rites of passage historically have been largely for men and supervised by men. As you search for elders to assist you in this ritual, however, remain open to calling upon both men and women, young and old. At the celebration during the incorporation phase, you will want to feel free to include all those people most important to you. Their gender or age probably won't be an issue for you.

You will want to tune each of the three phases to your own taste but here is a model for you to use:

Part I: Separation

Intent: To begin a transition from adulthood into the higher level of maturity—"eldership"—you need to let go of aspects of your sense of self and remain open to new ones. To assist in the process of transition to adulthood, the men of indigenous cultures, such as the Duk-duk in the Soloman Islands, would beat the initiate with sticks to ceremonially kill him. The lamenting mother would answer the initiate's cries of pain from a distance.[145] In the military the "recruit" is sent away from his community to boot camp where he is given a number and told to act like the others, forget his normal routine and develop personal habits forced on him by the drill instructor. The modern Western elder accomplishes the separation, however, through gentler means including affirmation, prayer and symbolic ceremony.

Questions: To let go of aspects of self and open yourself to others, the initiate would benefit from answering these questions:

1. How might I move from a selfish use of my time and resources to a service orientation?

2. In what ways can I address the issue of my own mortality?

3. Which of my life experiences have I framed darkly. Can I now reframe them with a positive view?

4. Who have I not forgiven? Am I wasting energy on resenting people who let me down a long time ago?

5. How can I let loose my grip and "just be" without loosing control?

6. Am I confident that I have wisdom?

7. Have I bought into the prejudice toward older people and do I believe my grey hair makes me useless?

8. In what way could I be a source of blessing to both man and the Earth?

9. Am I ready to move from *libido* drives like wealth, power and position into *thanatos* drives like service, contemplation, conservation and mentoring?

10. What am I resisting about balance in a fourfold way? Is my greatest challenge in the spiritual, intellectual, physical or psychological?

The Players: Most of the time in this initiation, the initiate will be alone. Gradually he will be encouraged to seek out other men he feels express eldership. This is covered in Parts II and III.

Ceremony: Enter the questions and your responses in a journal or diary. Journaling is an important element of your rite at all three stages. Journaling is one way to bring ceremony to the process of asking yourself the questions. To address the questions ceremonially, give an affirmative potential to your responses. Writing in a Journal is a tried and true method of imprinting new concepts. However, you may also want to add symbolic actions that express your intentions and mark this time of separation from your old ways.

Other examples of ceremony include burying or burning paper on which has been written those aspects of your life you are letting go. Some initiates create an alter or add to an existing one significant artifacts. In honor of the death that is separation, you and your ritual elder, or you alone, could go on a day long hike. During this time you could consider the questions. On the day of the walk try fasting until after sunset. Fasting symbolizes a cleansing and helps you reach atonement, *at-one-ment,* with nature. As you walk, observe how nature reaches out to you with signs and symbols of your life purpose, inherent gifts, personal values and fears. Look at the evidence of passage in fallen trees, trampled flora and dying leaves. Find a natural item that symbolizes your separation and bring it home.

Part II: Threshold

Intent: The intent of the threshold phase in the elder initiation is to incubate the future. Answers to the questions will coalesce to form a new foundation for a new mission of the elder. The difference between the threshold period in most people's lives and the threshold of the elder initiation is the maturity of the man seeking this ritual. Threshold is a time of education and training for initiates in other rites of passage. The man who is in the second half of life, however, has gathered much knowledge and has long life experience. Unlike the initiate who is joining a church as a young man or a boy who is passing through puberty, the elder will do most of his threshold training alone.

Once completing this phase, the elder will have a stronger feeling about what he is to do in the second half of life. This will, in turn, help him cope with the loss of what aspects of self he has had to sacrifice. Aimless wandering should begin, during the threshold, to become a more purposeful exploration of the responsibilities and potentials of elderhood. The possibilities of elder expression will overshadow the traditional older man's response of depletion, recreation and retirement.

The Players: Where, for example, the *catechumen* in the Catholic Church can depend on the priest to educate him during threshold, the elder must walk alone most of the time in his initiation. The catechumen, the neophyte Catholic, is usually young and lacks the experience of the elder. Elders can learn from others, but the goal in the elder threshold rite is to tap "the elder within." The other side of this issue is the difficulty in finding men who celebrate their elderhood. In the same way that I found men whom I called elders, I challenge the elder initiate to identify within his community at least three men who meet the following criteria: Do you know a man who

- Is seasoned, and a source of life-giving energy
- Knows his limitations and is skillful
- Has an unconquerable spirit
- Is knowledgeable, aware and filled with insight
- Is intuitive, passionate, spiritual and sensuous

The three can play a role in phase three but during threshold will be an important resource as well. Bounce the questions off these men and enter a discussion with each about your responses. You will likely find these North American elders shy and resistant, but pursue them. Once they learn that they play a role in supporting your quest for eldership, they will want to contribute something. The other player is the *ritual elder.*

During incorporation, the ritual elder will be your advocate and representative at the incorporation ceremony, but in threshold, utilize him as you would a good brother. Share your responses to the questions. Listen for his reactions as you will with the other three elders. The ritual elder's role in your rite is to facilitate the incorporation ceremony using the help of the other three. You will need to find a man who is comfortable with ritual and who is willing to facilitate. Consider a teacher, a thespian or a minister.

The key player in the threshold, however, is the elder initiate. Utilizing the stepping stones of wisdom, you will have to teach yourself how to become more elder-like. The stepping stones again are contemplation, listening, reflection and meditation. We need, therefore, to create ground for use of these tools and, at the same time, create sacred space.

In chapter one we reviewed the four aspects of initiation: community endorsement; sacred space; elder facilitation; the readiness of the initiate. You began forming sacred space in your walk in nature. Let's turn now to the ceremony of threshold. It is a sacred ceremony because the experience of it is utterly private, inexpressible and awesome. In this ceremony, the initiate is left alone with his perception of the universe.

Ceremony: To create ground for the stepping stones of wisdom, the elder initiate will now go on retreat. The form of this getaway is up to the initiate. It should last at least three days and three nights. The retreat will be in a place and done in a way that is sacred to the initiate. Sacred space is holy ground created when someone sees you, hears you, recognizes you and then admires and affirms you. Since the initiate will be alone, the only source of recognition and affirmation outside yourself will be your version of the universal force that organizes us all. The burden of creating sacred space in threshold, therefore, will be on the initiate utilizing prayer, affirmation or tools such as the stepping stones. The retreat could be a driving trip where you never settle in a particular place but spend most of your time alone on the road and in motels or camping grounds. For others it will mean traveling to a retreat center that invites people to stay for the purpose of contemplation and study. Others may want to leave people all together, camping in the wilderness if they have the skill.

Most ancient threshold rites of passage involved some hardship, risk or trial. The trial may be psychological or spiritual in nature. The initiate who would join a Christian church must repent "sins" he previously conceived to be nothing but "errors." He must declare he is ready to shift from involvement with self to a relationship with God, the nature of which is defined by an external force called "the Church." The catechumen cannot enter that part of the church building where communion or baptism takes place until he finishes the incorporation phase and is "confirmed." In some countries the catechumen faces rites of exorcism during threshold. Threshold can take two or three years in older tribal cultures such as those in Africa.

The military recruit endures a series of ordeals during threshold. These include trials of strength, sleeplessness, inspections, obstacle courses, battle practice, combat, and forced marches. Some cultures subject their initiates to tortuous rituals. In the Gulf of Guinea in the Congo of 1900, initiates into adulthood had their bodies mutilated and painted. Elders directed them to wander around in the forest naked and out of sight because during this part of their ritual they were presumed dead.

The elder will need to judge what role trial, challenge or risk will play in his ritual. Fasting again is recommended and is a trial for most, but the vessel cannot be filled until it is emptied. Threshold is a time of building new vision that fills the initiate. Journaling will nearly always enrich the process of transition. For some it is a challenge to put into words the things felt during initiation. Other terms for threshold in history have been *marge,* the French word for "margin," and the Latin, *liminal,* which means, "limit." In this phase the quester encounters his margin or limit of his former self and steps beyond. Indigenous people experience threshold not only as a time to move from one stage of life to another, but they also attribute to it a divinely sanctioned meaning. It enriches a man's life by relating him personally to the myths and spirits of his tribe. Trial for them, therefore, increases the reality of human frailty and encourages surrender to the "universal" from which neither man nor nature is separate.

Threshold ends when the elder initiate believes he has given sufficient time to the process of transition. This is artificial to some degree because the exact moment you complete a life change cannot be pinpointed. In three days and nights, you will have given yourself a good opportunity to contemplate the change, your past condition and your plans for the future. Those who utilize the vision quest, a rite similar to those practiced by Native Americans, spend at least three to four days in a wilderness place and make use of Native American artifacts and ritual believed to enhance the spiritual experience. The "questers" often report that they have experienced a "deathwarding birth contraction." When they rejoin their community they have a clearer understanding of themselves in relation to the natural environment, but also to the others to whom they return.[146]

The final act in threshold is to begin your return to your community. It is time to assess how an elder can act on his responsibility as an advocate for community. This is a good time to utilize the listening support of

145

your ritual elder. Your time away will have stirred things in you. You may want to share one of the secrets you have about yourself—one that you confronted on your time away. One way a person becomes personally linked with others is by opening up and sharing secrets. The last phase of this initiation involves your incorporation into your community. Any steps you can take that begin the process of melding with your circle of friends and relatives are worth experimenting with as the day of your incorporation ceremony approaches.

Part III: Incorporation

Intent: The goal of this final phase is to incorporate the initiate as *elder* through a celebration built on an endorsement from the people in the elder's community. He was a member of the community prior to his initiation as employer, brother, father, friend, teacher, spouse, neighbor or son. The ceremony of incorporation renews his membership in society now with the additional role of elder. The ceremony is usually an experience of renewal for the participants as well as the initiate. In this stage of their initiation, the aspiring church member is confirmed as an active member of the church. He is now given access to holy sacraments such as baptism and communion, a privilege reserved for confirmed members.

During incorporation, the military recruit is presented with clothing that makes him look the same as other members of the military—hence the name, *uniform.* He is given training that allows him to have an occupation. This allows him to play a specific role and in and on behalf of the community he has joined.

Players: At minimum, five persons are needed in the ceremony. In addition to the elder initiate, his ritual elder will be present to act as facilitator. The community will be standing in a large square during the ceremony. On each of the four sides a spokesperson will be asked to represent the community. If the initiate was able to identify a few elder men during the threshold phase, he may want to call on them as spokespersons.

For the four spokesperson's roles, the initiate will want people whom he trusts, who appreciate him and who are willing to step forward. This could include the initiate's children and spouse.

Ceremony: The initiate has some steps to take in preparation for the *incorporation* celebration. He will need to identify the players and confirm their willingness to act as spokespersons. He will then prepare a statement explaining what aspect of the self he will leave behind and what new characteristic he will adopt. Symbolically, *threshold* is a time of death—death of old ways of being. Incorporation is an opportunity to announce what it means to accept new ways—ways of eldership. The initiate will want to find someone in his community who can create a *mantle.* This could be a badge, a cloth wrap that hangs around the neck or even a garment. The ritual elder can advise the artist on the design. By accepting the mantle, the elder initiate symbolically accepts the responsibility and healing power of eldership. Finally, the initiate will define a method or ritual that will invoke the powers that are beyond himself. He could identify God or spirits meaningful to him, or people of his community, as his sacred energy source.

This issue of sacredness deserves further comment. In Van Gennep's review of worldwide rites of passage, he found that the initiate was not in his usual earthly state during the high points of the rites. The rituals possessed elements of intense sacredness because of the emotions and images they stirred in both the initiate and the people participating.

For each initiate the meaning of *sacred* differs. It usually is described as holy, religious, spiritual or divine. Invoking the influence of the sacred will usually be important to a man participating in the elder initiation, but each is free to judge this for himself. A man who does not consider himself spiritual can invoke the love and appreciation of his gathered friends and relatives.

While in the midst of the ritual, the initiate will experience a kind of rapture. The way he experiences it will vary depending on his religious and social heritage. A brief statement or set of behaviors will invoke the sacred. Either the initiate or the ritual elder can assume this responsibility.

On the day of the ceremony, all persons will stand on the outside of the square, the sides of which will be defined by the presence of the spokespersons. The ritual elder will walk the initiate to the center of the square, where he will remain. The square has historically symbolized stability and an established foundation. The four sides will represent the balance of the fourfold way: psychological; physical; spiritual; intellectual. They will also represent the four masculine archetypes of King, Lover, Warrior and Magician. And finally, they will represent four roles of eldership: *celebrant, conservationist, mentor, wisdomkeeper.*

In the east will stand the spokesperson for the Lover energy: youthfulness, playfulness and spirituality. The east symbolizes the elder's celebration of life and his role as he who blesses: *celebrant.* In the south, the spokesperson will stand for Warrior energy, assertiveness, and a commitment to high values that guides the elder as an advocate for people and the earth: *conservationist.* In the west the spokesperson will remind the elder that he who expresses Magician energy is a teacher and in service: mentor. The north side represents King energy. The spokesperson here announces that the community looks to the elder to be joyful in celebration of life and that he is responsible for utilizing his long life experience on behalf of younger generations. Each spokesperson will present one question for the elder initiate to answer spontaneously. The question is intended to provoke the initiate to consider each of the four elder roles.

As we approach the end of the ceremony, the initiate will be asked to speak. It is at this time that he will share a prepared statement about the meaning of the initiation to him. Also, he will have brought items discovered during the separation and threshold phases.

He must now in some way burn, bury or discard those that represent the past. Following this act of release, the ritual elder will bring forward the mantle of eldership and present it to the initiate. He will offer a blessing on behalf of the community and then request the persons gathered to approach the elder, offering touch, song or some other demonstrative form of endorsement that shows their pleasure with the incorporation of this elder.

The process of incorporating the man into the community is the responsibility of the elder's friends and relatives. Their presence at the ceremony is all that is needed. Hopefully, a number of these people have passed through their own threshold. They probably have not been through an elder initiation, but each stage of growth requires the steps of separation, threshold and incorporation. Everyone present will understand to some degree the importance of the ceremony, even if they have not been oriented to the idea. The gathered throng are "birth attendants, midwives."[147] The role of community will become even more important as we look at the work a man must do to grow into eldership.

Growing into Eldership

Growing into eldership probably will not happen just because you have lived a long life. The growth that is measured by reaching each stage of development is fourfold in nature, but my emphasis here is on psychological, intellectual and spiritual growth. We can mature and flower beyond our present state by choosing to grow. Once making this affirmation, we need to change attitudes, challenge biases and learn more information. We will need to evaluate our values. Our behaviors will, as a result, become different.

In what you have read so far, there are a number of hints about where we could focus our commitment to growth into eldership. I have asserted, for example, the importance of becoming balanced in a fourfold way. Carrying the mantle of eldership will be easier if we first solve our psychological problems, seek to become centered spiritually, keep better care of our physical health and study writers such as those quoted throughout this book. Elders express a compatible and balanced energy from each of the four masculine archetypes. This facilitates a positive expression of the three male roles of protector, provider and teacher. The full expression of masculine and feminine energy is another challenge. You will recall that Robert Bly asserts that the "integration" of these two energies is the last stage, the most mature stage, of personal development. An elder can grow in all these areas by committing to a review of the following attitudes, biases and expressions of values.

Myths About Aging

Our growth also requires that we stop clinging to our myths about aging. This includes confronting the *recreation—depletion—retirement* paradigm in the second half of life. Older people don't need less sleep than younger people but this is one our myths. Older men and women don't become sexless. People who don't follow the rule of maintaining young beauty appreciate "Elder beauty." Older people don't forget everything. "Of the 30 million Americans over the age of sixty-five, only 10 percent show any significant loss of memory."[148] The developmental task here is to overcome our inclination to let go of our youthfulness as we age. The wise elder retains his connection to youthful vitality. He balances libido and thanatos energy. Saint Augustine said, "Let your old age be childlike, and your childhood like old age; that is, so that neither may your wisdom be with pride, nor your humility without wisdom.[149] At each stage of life there is within us a coexisting presence of the child and the elder, the archetypal images of youth and age. Our negative images of aging result in large part from our denial that we retain libidinal drives, the youthful, spontaneous and resilient drives that continually bring adventure to life.

Accessibility

Elders need to be available. The problem with *recreation— depletion—retirement* is that we focus our energy on being occupied, frustrated and out-of-touch. Without a tradition of availability, older people assume their presence is unnecessary. They hit the road or move away from the extended family, thus reinforcing the myth that elders are less useful. Genuine wisdom is attributed to those with the "capacity to 'feel,'" to exhibit 'compassion' and 'generosity' toward others, and to develop intimate, insightful and empathetic relationships."[150] Building relationships requires regular exposure to those with whom you relate. Eldering is more an experience in being and less in doing. Elders needn't do anything while remaining within reach, but they must remain within reach. *Recreation—depletion—retirement* would look more like *harvesting—accepting our mortality—service* if being accessible were our goal. Rabbi Schacter says *in From Age-ing to Sage-ing,* that *harvesting* is a second half of life practice involving a celebration of the impact you have had in your lifetime. Harvesting then leads to a passion for leaving a legacy for the future.

Celebration

The second half of life is a time of celebration! What a wonderful influence this affirmation would have on us as we were growing up. Old age could be the time when we reap what we have sown. How about redefining *recreation* as re-creating through self-discovery, conservation of the earth or fostering the healthy growth of children! We can honor our *depletion* through improved health practices that could act as a reminder to stop doing so much and just be! A constructive form of *retirement* is centering through contemplation of all that we have sown, while at the same time staying in town more often and getting out so others can get a piece of us!

Celebration begins with a review of our life. When you are fifty years old, you can look back and see most of your life cycles. To have traveled through each stage of development is quite an accomplishment. The errors and omissions for which we are responsible can be reframed as "opportunities for growth." "The life review is…a progressive return to consciousness of past experience, in particular the resurgence of unresolved conflicts which can now be surveyed and integrated" into our enhanced elder sense of self.[151]

One of the most satisfying psychotherapeutic tools I have used in counseling is the task of "reframing." It requires a review of a portion of a person's life history that we find repugnant, and reevaluating the events by looking for hope and opportunity. Once discovering the doors that were opened for growth in each life experience, we can "reframe" the memory as a positive event. This literally allows us to reclaim energy previously devoted to calling past events negative or hurtful. Life review is more than recalling our past. We can heal the injury resulting from a trauma or disappointing life experience.

Painful memories affect how we act in the present when we endeavor to avoid experiences in the present that look like the painful ones of our past. We are often drawn into circumstances that are similar because we unconsciously want to heal the injuries and let go of our regret. Through the use of the wisdom tools of contemplation and meditation, we can recall the old memories and reframe them because of our maturity and readiness for celebration. A key to the process of reframing is forgiveness.

151

Forgiveness

In the second half of life a man "must come to terms with his grievances and guilts—his view of himself as victim and as villain...."[152] A man must not only accept his *shadow* but also forgive those people whose shadow victimized him. The elder is acquainted with his shadow but doesn't let it run his life. We can "acknowledge and assume responsibility for the damage we have incurred or caused. Working through [the resulting injury] calls for...healing forgiveness."[153] Rudyard Kipling wrote in this exerpt from his poem, *If:*

> *If neither foes nor loving friends can hurt you;*
> *If all men count with you, but none too much;*
> *If you can fill the unforgiving minute*
> *With sixty seconds' worth of distance run—*
> *Yours is the Earth and everything that's in it,*
> *And—which is more—you'll be a Man my son!*

To not forgive is to invest present energy in things past. Holding a grudge is work that wastes present day resources on history. The man who let you down isn't even aware of how much work you put into remembering what you call "his unforgivable act." In my training with the Spiritual Eldering Institute (1997-98), we did an exercise called "A Testimonial Dinner for My Severe Teachers." As we do life review, specific people are remembered darkly. The trainer asked us "What if you invited your lifelong enemies to an imaginary banquet?" In the spirit of reframing, then, we made a list of the guests we would invite. Next to each guest's name, we listed what he or she did that was so difficult. Finally, next to each difficulty, we listed its benefit. We looked for the unexpected gift in the acts of the enemies on our list. Finally, we forced ourselves to write down something about the difficulty for which we are now grateful. In this exercise we did not have to forgive the guests. *Forgiveness* in this case was the name we gave to finally giving up the burden of anger or hurt which had kept us in the role of victim.[154]

Forgiving is more involved than excusing. It is a way to save energy for use in the second half of life. For the wise elder forgiveness is an empathetic healing of memory. Wisdom allows the elder to recognize his severe teachers as victims themselves. He enters into the pain that he has caused others through a misuse of power or uncontrolled anger. Through such empathy, a cleansing takes place. He then forgives hurt without harboring resentments and frees himself from the energy-consuming bitterness of holding a grudge.

Confronting Our Mortality

In my criticism of the paradigm of traditional aging, *recreation— depletion—retirement,* I do not mean to suggest a denial of depletion. Our *preoccupation* with depletion concerns me. One day I rode Amtrak between Portland, Oregon and Tucson, Arizona. A man in his seventies and I struck up a stimulating conversation about family, work and other things meaningful to both of us. Another man sat down at our table a short time later. He was also of my new friend's generation. Soon the two men began an endless conversation about the physical ailments they had experienced. Their engrossment with their experience of depletion overwhelmed and replaced our earlier discussion. In a way, each man made himself inaccessible to me by dwelling on his fear of mortality.

For men in particular, the challenge of confronting mortality is to convert our life long commitment to "kill and survive" to an attitude of "die and become."[155] German poet and novelist Johann Goethe wrote:

> *Die and Become.*
> *Till thou hast learned this*
> *Thou are but a dull guest*
> *On this dark planet.*

Mortals must face death, but the process takes longer and longer as time passes. Depletion is real yet gradual. If we tap the rhythm of elderhood, it influences us to slow down and listen to deeper impulses and question the hectic pace of youth. In Mitch Albom's, *Tuesdays With Morrie,* the terminal older man, Morrie, says to his interviewer, "Well, the truth is, if you really listen to that bird on your shoulder—*if you accept that you can die at any time*—then you might not be as ambitious as you are…. The things you spend so much time on—all this work you do—might not seem as important. You might have to make room for some spiritual things."[156]

Morrie utilized his impending death as a teaching tool. By reflecting deeply on our impermanence, we can be energized in the present because we accept that we must deal with the contingency of time. Morrie's acceptance of his mortality helped move him toward elderhood. He energized himself to share his wisdom, *now!* People who have had near-death experiences often have a reduced fear of and deeper acceptance of mortality. It is common for them to have an increased interest in service, an enhanced grasp of the importance of love. They lose interest in materialistic objectives because "you can't take it with you."

The specter of death beckons us to move into the elder stages of development. If elders don't face depletion and death directly, they find themselves in a trap resisting the flow of time. In my Spiritual Eldering work, we call this, "the box of unlived life." On one side of the box is the future. To move into the future, we must accept our mortality. Most of us fear this reality, however, causing us to look away, to look back into the past. The past is on the other side of the box. If we haven't reframed our failures and disappointments, we don't want to face them. We are then forced to live within the box, without the ability to look toward the future and view our past with poise and confidence.[157]

Though I believe that death will be the most powerful experience in my life, western culture works hard to help me deny my imminent death. Media and advertising try to cultivate a belief in immortality, because this is what we are interested in buying. Most human fear is rooted in our fear of death. Life can scare us because of its unpredictability. In my quest for elderhood, I keep studying death, dying and mortality. This study is at least more productive than an outright denial of my death, but I have a long way to go in accepting the rhythm of death in life. I believe in the importance of confronting my mortality because of my belief in both the spiritual realm and in the task of conserving energy in the second half of life. My spirituality includes the belief that life is eternal through the medium of the soul. Energy conservation is served by not investing too much of my might in fear of things over which I have little control.

Developing Confidence in Your Wisdom

From chapter one, the reader will recall my reference to the energy in the psyche as the *elder within*. Once we access this energy actively, we can be elder-like. My description of an elder may feel more like an aspiration than a real possibility, but there is within us "elder potential." The elder within has been conceptualized by the Spiritual Eldering Institute as your 120 year-old self. The Bible gives 120 years as the "age of wisdom." The elder within is the archetype of our fully-realized self who has done his life review and forgiveness work, who has let go his biases about aging, faced his mortality and integrated libido and thanatos energy. He is my source of hope that I will become an elder.

Try this exercise taught to me by the Institute. Record the following on audiotape so that you can play it back to guide yourself through the imagery. As a man seeking a fuller expression of eldership, you will need to contact your inner source of wisdom and receive occasional guidance. This is your elder within who resides in your heart and exists beyond time and space. You can visit with your ancient, fully-actualized self and obtain reassurance whenever you need it. Because your elder within exists at age 120, he can guide you with knowledge of your future. In this guided meditation you can make an appointment to visit your elder within at any time. To begin this exercise, find a quiet place to sit.

The Exercise

Become aware of your breathing. Don't change the rhythm of it but become more aware of your in-breath and your out-breath. Now, begin counting from your current age up to 120. As you count, picture yourself walking up a flight of stairs that lead to a door. Once reaching the door, knock on it and enter. You are greeted with a warm hug by your evolved spiritual self, your *elder within*. Gaze into his eyes and experience unconditional love and reassurance about your progress in life. Ask your elder within for guidance about a specific concern with which you have been grappling. After asking, quietly remain receptive to his response and allow it to imprint itself on your consciousness. Turn off the tape recorder for awhile.

When you receive your answer, turn on the recorder once again. Look once more into the eyes of this inner grandfather and hear these parting words, "Journey on with confidence and with blessings as you proceed on your path. Visit me again whenever you need further guidance." Bid him goodbye, turn and walk through the door, down the steps slowly and return to your point of departure—your present chronological age. Sit quietly for a few moments. Open your eyes when you are ready. Turn off the recorder. You can now return regularly to visit your inner elder and be reassured of your gifts and wisdom. *(End of exercise.)*

To develop confidence in your wisdom, first ask yourself, "What choice do I have?" Wisdom is insight and intuition synthesized through love and hope. You contain your fears and shyness about speaking your mind when sharing wisdom. The wise man is more concerned with being accessible than being verbal, however. If I remain inaccessible and quiet, for fear that my long life experience has yielded little wisdom, maybe I will waste something needed by others. Second, make lists of all your roles: father; worker; community leader; voter; hobbyist; maintenance man around the home; husband; entrepreneur; traveler; pet owner; etc. Then list next to each role how many years you have been playing each. Now add up the years. This extensive experience could benefit others if shared. The task of experimenting with and provoking social change, and developing new ideas and tools is assigned to the young. How efficiently can they progress without the support of the elders?

Finally, don't fear that your interference will cause a repetition of old ways and discourage creativity. We "have to enlist the elders, who have traditionally been the wardens of culture, to help and guide us in the vital process of reversing deculturation and of crafting the new myths on which reculturation can be based."[158] The young are vigorous and will not allow a return to ways and methods no longer useful, but they lack the memory of better days and a greener earth. The elder of today remembers when families were more functional, when no freeways existed, when you could cut down a Christmas tree near your home. The elder remembers when childcare was not an industry but rather an occasional need, when fathers stayed with their families and women didn't have babies out of wedlock. We may not return to those experiences, but the memory of them influences the elder.

Loosening Your Grip

Growing into eldership is spiritual work. Spiritual work involves seeking the meaning of life. The elder is a seeker and is thus on a spiritual journey that "grows him up." The key to spiritual work is "Letting Go and Letting God." This requires letting go our grip on our ego, that aspect of self that is not immortal. The spirit is immortal. Once letting go your ego, you need then to come to the understanding that you are a servant of a higher purpose than self. Once letting go of your grip on your ego, you are left with a bit of a void and discovering that higher purpose helps you fill it. The *loosening of our grip* causes a movement away from individualism and toward union with the community and nature. In our youth we feed our ego. In eldership we honor our ego but experience ourselves as one of many egos in an interrelated human community. A synergy occurs between elders and community that energizes both.

The concept of loosening our grip is considerably different than "losing your grip!" One aspect of our mortal reality in the second half of life is the gradual diminishment of our physical prowess. Our hand's grip may diminish as well, but this is also quite different than loosening your grip. There is no reason for a healthy older man to diminish intellectually or psychologically. In fact, the ability to loosen your grip is proof of increased intellectual and psychological growth. The balanced man is a good "stress manager." Effective stress managers understand above all else how much they can handle. Concerning what they can't handle, they loosen their grip a bit. This allows them to use their given pool of energy for just those challenges within their energy range.

To loosen your grip interpersonally means, for example, to take criticism from others less seriously. The elder knows that criticism is discriminating judgment, not condemnation. To loosen your grip psychologically means, in part, to loosen up about fears by letting them pass on through. Fears take a toll when we hold onto them, letting them take us out of our center, our spirit. To loosen your grip philosophically, stop asking "why" and follow your heart with confidence in your wisdom. To loosen your grip in parenting is to stay within reach of your children but to get "out of their face." They are probably adults who need *you,* but not your instruction.

He of the loosened grip, while not losing control, is more relaxed. Being relaxed brings about qualities like patience, clearer perception, a present focus and a desire to listen and talk less. He of the loosened grip utilizes *discernment,* the most valuable of the virtues among mystics. Mystics, like the holy men reviewed in chapter three, are "keen on the *experience* of the Divine and will not settle for theory alone or *knowing about* the Divine." [159] Discernment is an experience of the divine. To be discerning is to sense the sacred in other people by connecting to them through your spirit, your soul.

When you sit with an elder who is discerning, you will find him deeply attentive to you. Because he has let go his tight hold on many lesser things, he gathers additional energy he can use to be open, patient and permeable to all you are saying. The discerning elder follows his intuition about what to do with what he has perceived in you. The discerning elder can not only put himself out of the way so he can hear you, but he can also help you develop and trust in your own powers of discernment. This virtue "is a sort of sanctified common sense…It sees the humorous side of exaggeration…"[160] You have to loosen your grip before you can see the humorous side of things.

Balancing Our Psychic Energies

Those influences that emanate from our psyche I call the "energies," both conscious and unconscious, make up the human personality. In chapter four, I discussed those energies that weigh heavily in determining mature masculine expression. They include: the four archetypes—King, Lover, Warrior and Magician; the masculine and feminine energies; shadow energy; and the energy from each of the three male roles—protector, provider and teacher of cultural tradition. Growing into eldership includes utilizing these psychic influences in a way that is balanced or most healthy. A "balance of expression" of the four archetypes results in a mature manifestation of healthy masculinity. A "controlled expression" of shadow energy, on the other hand, is the goal of the wise elder.

There are "bright energies" and "shadow energies" common to the psychic imprint, or inborn pattern of expression, for each masculine archetype. The task in maturity is to draw upon each of the four and also to keep under control the destructive shadow energy of each. A man who expresses himself utilizing bright King energy, for example, is generative and celebrates new life in a joyful way. The King's shadow side would move the man to be destructive in his fear of new life. It is from the dark side of this archetype that a man expresses patriarchy and is willing to degrade others. Growing into eldership, then, includes an attempt to express bright masculine energy as much as possible.

Lover energy brings about a playful and sensuous approach to living. At his best, the man expressing bright Lover energy is intuitive and spiritual. He is in touch with the Oneness of all men and connects us all through feeling. Shadow Lovers lack boundaries, however, and disrespect those of others. Do you see the dance here between the bright side and the shadow side of an archetype? In a healthy expression, Lover means connection. In an unhealthy expression, it means over-connection as we forget to respect other people's need to be private.

Magician energy brings about the healer in us and stimulates the teacher in us. The Magician is the master of knowledge and in his concrete view of the world can protect us from the emotional irrationality of the Shadow Lover. Each archetype can protect us from the shadow of the other three. The Shadow Magician is manipulative, slippery and illusive. He is known as the Trickster in mythical history. He can be dishonest and lets his fears determine his reactions to people.

The Warrior, on his best days, is assertive in his quest to reach lofty goals that take him beyond selfishness. Warrior energy is good for us as it causes us to establish safe boundaries, thus protecting us from the manipulative shadow Magician or the tyranny of the shadow King. The shadow Warrior perpetrates violence and can be sadistic and cowardly. The uncontrolled anger of this archetype abuses women and children and is feared by other men. The adult man of the twenty-first century is more confused about this archetype than the other three. In our attempt to grow away from patriarchy, many of us have confused shadow King energy with the assertiveness that comes from Warrior energy. As we relax our exploitative, patriarchal ways, we have mistakenly laid down the Warrior sword that has been essential in the protection of mankind.

Balancing our masculine and feminine energies requires an honoring of both. The twenty-first century elder respects that he has both feminine and masculine traits, while at the same time understanding that gender expression changed considerably in the twentieth century. He understands that while seeking power is a masculine "trait," more women today express masculine power-seeking "energy."

The man who is in the second half of life is more likely to be contemplative than he has when younger. This is a feminine trait. The use of power has changed in the past few decades. Men used to be identified with political and economic power, women with emotional and sexual power. Now, increasing numbers of professional women and increasing numbers of child-rearing men have both changed our view of masculine and feminine power expression.

Some things also seem never to change about men and women. "The woman…is experienced…as the source and giver of life…whereas the male… is one who *gained* his powers…The mother is experienced as a power of nature and the father as the authority of the society…."[161] Honoring the masculine and the feminine includes considering the question, "Aren't some expressions or gender roles hard-wired into the psyche of both men and women?" I don't know the answer but I am convinced that the elder has grappled with the question.

Growing into eldership requires confronting our compulsions, weaknesses and addictions. This is our dark side, our human challenge. We are not just holy spirits. We are angels on the human journey as well as humans on a spiritual journey. The dark side of humanity is what I introduced in chapter one as the *shadow*. This is that part of us of which we are not proud. The shadow energies expressed by each of the four masculine archetypes must be contained to some degree. These are the aspects of the *self* that you need to monitor, for they can cause you to express destructive compulsive and addictive behaviors.

An elder learns that people project their shadow onto others in trying to pretend they have no dark side. Test this by considering what behaviors or personality characteristics you like least in other people. An objective explanation for why you don't like people acting in those ways is that you don't like observing your shadow. What we disapprove of in others' behaviors we don't enjoy in ourselves. Otherwise, why would we be so invested in other people's ways of being?

The elder enters into a dance with his shadow. This dance allows the shadow some expression, but it doesn't take control. Shadow energies only become destructive when they are not honored. In the elder's dance with shadow, he absorbs the shadow's power and doesn't attempt to repress it. This absorption converts shadow energy into a vitality that is stimulating but still potentially risky. If absorbed, it is neither repressed nor expressed. Try to imagine manipulation, anger or compulsion expressed at a low level of energy. Absorbed shadow energy can be invigorating. The elder continues the dance throughout his life.

Balancing our psychic energies includes, finally, the living out of twenty-first century male roles. I have narrowed the list down to three: protector, provider, and teacher of cultural tradition. To assist the aspiring elder in this balancing act, let's use chapter six to review these roles in action.

❖   ❖   ❖   ❖

Don, an elder with over sixty years life experience
An elder is a man who became wise by being unwise,
Acquired judgment by being foolhardy

In the Mankind Project, a men's organization to which I belong, Don is considered one of the original elders. Only men over the age of fifty-five are assigned the role of "ritual elder" within the organization. This position requires maturity. Most of all, the man in this role is to be a model of spirituality in action during the weekend gatherings the organization sponsors. A number of years ago, Don began to conceptualize what it meant to be an elder. His commitment to the mental health and welfare of the other men in the Mankind Project led him to lead the original thinking that defined the elder role. Men listen to Don because he is trusted. When you are in his presence you feel warm. He offers grandfather love and strength in its best form. Here are some of the things Don believes about generative adult men.

They have lived out most of the challenges of life and have a cumulative wisdom about the human journey. The elder, of whom Don speaks, has an "inner life." He has an inner intimacy with his psychic world and its energies and patterns. This generative older man has faced his dragons—the self-destructive and harmful aspects of his shadow. He has gained some containment of them but he knows the struggle is never complete. Don believes that the elder has discovered a mythic dimension to life and is, therefore, acquainted with stories and heroes of his culture. He shares deeper insights out of this acquaintance with myth and story. The ritual elder, Don says, believes in the power of ritual in the creation of sacred space. He is able to lead other men in the creation and sustaining of a ritual container of sacred energies.

The elder is a mentor of younger men. He is able to see their beauty and power. Don feels that the mentor should help younger men see and realize their own golden potential. He is also able to see ways in which younger men sabotage their potential. His job is to help them face the challenge of learning how they get in their own way. The generative older man has the power of blessing with which he can help to heal a damaged self-image and confirm in men a stronger belief in themselves. The elder, Don believes, has come to grips with the inevitability of his death and has found a way of both accepting and transcending it through the power of vision and trust. This man has an earnest concern for the quality of life on this planet. He wants to protect and preserve the environment. He wants to re-order society creatively so that future generations can realize their full potential.

Chapter VI

ACTION ELDERHOOD

Men hungering for father,
Heart in hand
Try to allow me into your space
Briefly or for years, I a
Mentor be, only at your calling
Be blessed calls the elder.

In the early part of 1990, I turned fifty years old. In February of that year, I had ventured with sixty other people to a spiritual retreat on a Pacific island. We were housed in rustic facilities at a retreat center set in a jungle area. Just across the road was the ocean. Having lived on the Pacific coast of the USA for most of my life, I was acquainted with the ocean. But I had not, until then, been on a relatively small body of land surrounded by the great body of water . The island was volcanic. Within two miles of our location, a flow of molten lava was pushing unyieldingly down the mountainside towards the sea. I was surrounded for ten days with unfamiliar flora, fragrances completely new to me, and animal and insect life that intimidated me. It was in this place, at this time, that I made a leap in my spiritual journey. I believe that I needed isolation in a place where the energy of the earth was overwhelming so that I might discover my reason for being. This is the purpose of a spiritual journey.

It wasn't a curiosity about my reason for being, however, that moved me to begin this journey. I had, for a number of years, been feeling empty, and I lacked depth. I had very little spark to get me going each day. The emptiness inside me needed filling. I had a wonderful wife and family, professional success and good health, but the emptiness was overwhelming. I sensed that there was more. What I was experiencing was a primal feeling of separation from a place deep within me—my soul. My first step on the pathway to elderhood was to confront the separation. What began that week in 1990, as I ended midlife and entered maturity, was a conversion to a belief in purpose. Either we are here, in this existence, for some reason, or we pass through life simply by accident. I began confronting life from my heart, the doorway to the soul. I began questioning my shadow uncontrollably and the damage I did when it ran my life. I started to shift away from "doing" toward a contemplative experience of "being." Elders, I came to believe, are on a nearly unmanageable and involuntary spiritual journey.

The Elder's Spiritual Journey

Because the second half of life today is considerably longer than it ever was before, we should ask if this longevity has a purpose. Longer life is a blessing that allows more time to ask questions, more time with family, and more time to play. It leaves more "time to drink wine, to eat bread not by yourself but by some other magic."[162] Spiritual teachers of history have taught that our presence here is more than biological and coincidental, and that to manifest our true being requires a spiritual journey. Most soulful philosophers teach us that the purpose of living on earth is to achieve union with our essential nature. Our essential nature is our spirit, the aspect of man that connects us to one another and to the divine. Both the earth and mankind are healed somewhat every time someone advances on their spiritual journey.

Watching an elder in action is observing a balanced, generative and modern form of mature masculinity. An elder plays out the three male roles in a way that demonstrates a fourfold approach to living in the twenty-first century. I believe that the crowning expression of the fourfold approach is the spiritual one. Possessing psychological, intellectual and physical health is essential to a man's experience of being. Being spiritual, however, connects the man to all the rest that makes up wholeness: people;

the Earth; and God or whatever unifying force ties it all together for you. The only way to remain spiritually alive is to express your spirit actively. This brings me back to elders and the three male roles of protector, provider and teacher. As a man seeks to maintain his journey and grow in eldership, he finds himself modeling maturity and mentoring, if only occasionally and in small ways.

Eastern/Western Spirituality

The elder facilitates the march of other men down their spiritual path by modeling soulful expression both among men and in the Earth. Buddhists, believing spiritual masters are enlightened beings, say that attaining liberation from the ego and its fear-induced lifestyle, and to reach enlightenment, is only possible by following a spiritual model—the master. A spiritual master is a person who expresses eldership in the eyes of his disciples. One Buddhist priest said about the influence of his master on the disciple's pathway, "The sun's rays fall everywhere uniformly, but only where they are focused through a magnifying glass can they set dry grass afire."[163] The master is the disciple's magnifying glass.

Buddhists believe that the adoration of your master, your teacher, brings the disciple closer to becoming an elder himself. Therefore, the disciple's admiration is largely an affirmation, an attempt to make the spiritual teacher an elder. When the disciple's devotion to the master brings the disciple to the point where he literally believes the master to be nothing less than the Buddha himself, the disciple is ready to become a master—a type of elder. The challenge for an elder is to become a seeker and, therefore, to model the way of the wayfarer. In this way, like the spiritual guide, the elder, is *holding the container* for the disciple. The concept of a spiritual guide has all but disappeared in the West, but the challenge to become an elder and to express eldership remains. Today's long life experience is a challenge to eldership. The need for wisdom in the community and in the family is a challenge to eldership.

The Westerner's naivete about gurus and elders of other world traditions leads one to believe that eldering means "seeking out a high mountain cave and becoming contemplative with limited human contact." The fascination some have with "wise men" around the world suggests an image of elder as reclusive. Even Buddhists, however, in their nearly irrational admiration of spiritual teachers, assume the elder in their life is going to be accessible. What good is an inaccessible teacher? In the Islamic tradition called the *Sufi*, an elder is expected to prove one's love for humanity in part by interacting with people and being accessible to them. The Sufis don't believe that their spiritual teachers are perfect in the way Buddhists do, but they expect the teacher to show "mother-spirit, the father-spirit, the brother-spirit, the child-spirit, the friend-spirit...an ever tolerant nature...compassion [and a] thorough understanding of human nature."[164] These are still classy credentials, however, especially for people of the West. The two keys to the elder's credibility, in a western, Buddhist or Sufi tradition are:

1. his willingness to be available, and

2. the devotion of the student. It is the synergy with one's student that completes the teacher.

Male Eldering

In this chapter, we will look at *eldering*, the spirit-centered soul-nourishing behavior of people in the second half of life devoted to converting *recreation—depletion—retirement* into *harvesting—accepting our mortality—service*. At the basis of eldering is the devotion to being available to younger generations. A twenty-first century expression of the three male roles *must* be influenced by the same principles. An expression of provider, protector and teacher that is spiritual will not only empower others, but also protect the elder from the impoverishment of soul that these roles have historically caused.

For example, few male behaviors have had as serious an impact on the psyche, physique and soul of men as the manner in which we carry out the role of provider. It began with a man's desire to supply his dependents with food, garb and shelter so that he would in turn have company, sex and progeny. It evolved into soul-ravaging work for wages performed in business and industry that could easily become the first reason for his existence, remove him from his family and keep him permanently off the land. As we look at a mature expression of masculinity, then, what does "provider" mean for the spiritual elder who is finished with the corporate world, hungering to return to family and, once again, sees the beauty of the land? To answer this, we need to return briefly to the two life instincts—libido and thanatos.

When I first studied the libido and its drives, I assumed that the libido begins to die in the second half of life. It was at this time, I thought, that the completing and contemplative instincts of thanatos replace the libido. A problem arose, however. A number of large, stressful and action-oriented challenges came into my life when I passed the age of fifty. I shifted from my professional occupation into an occupation with this book and the research that went into it. I had to let go of my children as they matured and moved into their adult lives. My wife took off professionally. At age fifty, she was as vigorous and passionate about her work as I had been in my thirties. While I was gradually resting into a quieter and less aggressive style of living, I was also charged with new passions, new relationships and new activities that came with these new charges. My libido was elevated in some ways and was calmed in others. At fifty, I was beginning to be drawn by the siren call of thanatos, but it would be many years before contemplation, reminiscing, meditation, listening and quiet days of minimal anxiety would be mine.

Action Versus Elderhood

What then is "action elderhood?" Are "action" and "elder" contradictory? Elder action does not resemble the energetic and decisive "man of action" archetype that our culture celebrates. It includes, however, the playful and lighthearted grandfather who is still a learner and can be found celebrating life with friends or sitting in the forest in a beam of sunshine, just because. The elder asked the student why he was in the history class.

"I need to. It is a requirement," says the student.

"Why do you want to satisfy the requirements?" continued the elder.

"I want to have a college degree," he says.

"Why?"

"So I can get a job."

"And....?"

"And earn some money."

"The money is for.....?"

"Travel, I love to travel."

"Oh, yes. I love to travel too and I do," smiles the elder.

The Action Elder spends less time on the means to an end like he used to. He moves toward that which has inherent satisfaction. Action elderhood is behavior that:

- pleases inherently
- empowers others
- conserves nature
- blesses the young
- honors the energy pool in the elder's aging body
- makes good use of the elder's long life experience

Being an Action Elder can require activity, but it is also "useless" in some ways, like a large weeping willow tree, the tallest mountain in the range or the Grand Canyon. These sources of inspiration do nothing, yet they are sources of blessing and awe-inspiring beauty. They are models of serenity and strength. In their size they dwarf and place in perspective our worries and fears. Could action elderhood mean spending useless time with others? Time not to *do* but rather to just *be?* Time to be a good listener and time to ask others important questions like, "Is your life working out the way you hoped?" "How are you feeling?" "Would you like to just sit quietly with me?" This is the quality of being accessible. Those for whom we could become a resource may need nothing more than someone capable of giving them attention.

Both the *useless elder* and the Action Elder can be resources. The useless elder blesses by giving attention. Recall the meaning of sacred space: *holy ground created when people are both seen and heard, recognized, admired and affirmed by another.* How do you explain the magic that occurs between the attending grandfather and the granddaughter? The relationship between the child and her parents is distorted by the multiple demands of raising her and her need to form her personality, often achieved by contrasting with her parents' deficiencies. As grandparent, I can be wonderfully useless and waste time with my granddaughter whom I adore. I can see so clearly because I am not overinvested in how she develops. If we are quiet, willow trees or mountains of patience either for our grandchildren, friends or simply the clerk at the store, we need not fade away as we age because people will gather beneath our shade.

PROVIDER

The twenty-first century provider, who is a good example of the mature masculine in action, is one who endows, not just supplies. He accommodates, not simply furnishes. He contributes while he fills up, and he replenishes those he serves. Let us look now at action elderhood and the provider role together. The way the elder endows is by his accessibility.

Giving Attention, Being Accessible

One of my mentors once told me that older people, in trying to be accessible, often get so impatient to "upload" by sharing with younger people that they forget the secret of mentoring: don't try to be a mentor! "Once the word gets out that someone has good ears," he said, " young people will come. It's like fishing. If you yank at the first nibble, the fish gets off the hook." I experimented with this idea by first asking myself what is the simplest form of being accessible and giving attention at the same time. I decided that it begins with strangers on the street. Daily, I set sacred intention by lighting a candle on my altar at home. I affirm that during the day I will give gratitude for grace in my life and look for ways to affirm life. This is the process ancient elders call a daily experience in "the blessing way." Finding ways to affirm life is not easy, so I look for simple ways to do it.

Giving attention to a stranger affirms life. It would be easy if every day some person came up to me and asked for help with some personal crisis. You can even drive the streets and, many times, find someone with a flat tire or someone needing directions. Helping these people is an example of affirming life. So is weeding your garden or contributing money to a conservation cause. Again, I was looking for the simplest form of giving attention and decided that it could happen by greeting strangers more readily. Emanating friendliness, courage and a desire to be available, the elder can be action- oriented by seeking to say, "Hello" first and offering the first smile to others. In this way, he takes on the responsibility for offering a blessing and making the day a little less difficult for others. He may make the first step in creating a dialogue with someone who needs his wisdom.

Facilitate Community

Keep in mind that we are creating a new way of being in the role of "provider." A soul-nourishing way to provide for, to endow and to fill up others is to improve the community in which they live. Our world begins with self, and then we are members of a community either in the form of family, neighborhood, social group or workplace. From community the world moves up to city, state, country, world, universe. The elder is more likely to have an impact on our country and world by facilitating community. The young that he has raised are in charge now of the other building blocks of our world. So, keeping it simple, let's look at what action elderhood's potential impact on the community could be. Start with your neighborhood or your apartment building.

Let's walk along and observe the spiritual elder in his community. He has surveyed the area, remaining open to possibilities for affirming life. He observes, for example, that his neighbors all have their own lawnmowers, video cameras, bicycles and barbecues, and seldom think about sharing their use. It is unlikely, he muses, that any single neighbor knows the names of more than a few of his fellow community members. Nearly all of his neighbors use babysitters that they bring in from other neighborhoods. This is elder data we will return to below.

Arriving at the park on the corner, the elder comes upon a teenager playing basketball. What possibilities for building community lie in this situation? The elder catches the boy's eye and says,

"Hello, don't you live on Aaron Court?"

"Yea," he says, a little shy.

"The Hewett's live there. They used to live on our street," says the elder.

"They have a house next to ours," the boy reports as he once again shoots the ball.

"They have a boy your age don't they?" asks the elder.

"No, the girl that lives there is my age," says the boy.

"I am Terry Jones. We live on Stonehaven Court," offers the older man.

"Hi," says the boy.

As he begins to walk away, the elder says, "I sure hope the rain doesn't disturb your play. Have a good day." The boy waves and smiles partly because an older man has noticed him. Neighbors the boy has not met usually say nothing. This was a simple yet different experience in community facilitated by the older man. Who knows what might happen the next time the boy and the elder meet? The boy found the older man approachable and interested in him. Sacred space was created.

The elder then approaches a neighbor across the street attempting to edge his lawn with a hand tool. The elder approaches, greets the neighbor and offers to loan his power weed-wacker for this job. The neighbor, a little caught off-guard, hesitates and then accepts the offer. Later when the neighbor returns the weed-wacker, the two men find themselves planning to buy a power washer together. They come to the conclusion that each of them needn't buy equipment alone when they can split the cost. The elder suggests that they expand the agreement. If either man ends up moving out of the community, he will receive a fair cash settlement for his ownership and leave the machine in the community. They both assume that other neighbors may like to use the power washer. The expanded relationship between the two men results in the neighbor's expanded passion for sharing with other neighbors as well. Sacred space has allowed the holy practice of service. The following week, the neighbor offers to power-wash the slippery sidewalk of the single mother across the cul-de-sac.

He explains to the elder that since the woman works, one of her greatest challenges is finding adequate childcare. During the day she takes her children to a day care center. The remainder of the time she must often use unfamiliar babysitters so that she can get away occasionally. After confirming with his wife, the elder later visits the single mother and offers his home as a safe place for her children to stay whenever she is in a pinch. The following year, the woman and her children celebrate Thanksgiving with the elder and his wife. The children's grandparents live across the country and seldom are capable of visiting. Sacred space, once created, can also end up feeling like a home away from home.

Connect to others. Share with others. Serve others. This facilitates the *action* of community. "To commune" originally meant to make intimate connections with others. Once this intimacy exists, the people in the connection begin to set standards for living with one another that make possible the highest standard of living. When people join the community, they receive the blessing of the intimately connected group. Is the Jewish boy truly confirmed if no one attends his *bar mitzvah?* Is a person really married if the ceremony of marriage does not include an endorsement from one's community? Entering into intimate connection with others completes us. Can a human being raised from birth by wolves ever develop a human personality? Can we grow into full personhood without seeing ourselves reflected in the response of others? The core of community is the functional family.

Advocate for Family

Families need glue to hold them together. Both extended and nuclear families are being threatened with extinction. Not more than thirty-five years ago the number of American children living apart from their biological fathers was 17 percent of the total.[165] A first marriage today has only a 50 percent chance of survival. Fatherlessness caused by births out-of-wedlock almost equals in number that caused by divorce. One kind of glue that is missing in family is father and grandfather energy. Men have an irreplaceable role to play in child development, and no social unit is more necessary in a healthy culture than the family. Grandfathers can do at least two things to strengthen the family:

1. Maintain a commitment to the woman in their life as a model;
2. Be accessible to their grandchildren, especially those whose father is distant.

Involved biological fathers are deeply caring and selfless toward their children. This kind of father energy can't be transferred easily. Grandfathers have more of this energy than any other man, including stepfathers. Ample evidence exists that genetic fathers are more committed to their children than any other men.

I sincerely apologize to the wonderful stepfathers many of us have known. My assertion about involved genetic fatherhood is meant to emphasize the importance of genetic grandfathers. I don't want to show disdain for involved stepfathers, but rather encourage grandfathers to follow their hearts directly into the arms of their children's children. Our bias against older people has allowed them to lose confidence in their grandparent potential. The family needs this energy. Remember, to reach elder levels of maturity requires an expression of generativity—an active concern for others beyond the members of one's nuclear family and for younger generations in general. The personal benefits are measurable. The happiest group of men in North America has been found to be those over age fifty living with their mate in the "empty nest."[166] Could it be in part because they have access to grandchildren in a way that is both generative and delightful, and they get to see this in the eyes of the child?

The family changes as society changes, not the reverse. Urban society has intruded forcefully on the family, taking over many functions that were once the province of the family. The family is relinquishing the job of socialization of children earlier and earlier. Schools, mass media and the peer group are taking over the guidance and education of children. But society has not developed adequate sources of socialization and support to replace that which the family has relinquished. At the same time, conditions that allow or require both spouses to work outside the home create situations that can heighten and exacerbate conflict between the spouses. Action elderhood is now more necessary than ever!

I remain within reach of my adult children. It is no longer right for me to be an "in your face parent," but our interdependence makes it necessary for both child and parent to be accessible, available upon request. "Action grandparenting," then, includes supporting both your adult children and their children. With my children's permission, I can play a role in childcare, for example. A grandparent can loan money to facilitate an adult child's movement from one stage of life to another. Elder grandparents can take responsibility for maintaining family traditions like the Christmas wreath on the front door, annual trips to the pumpkin patch before Halloween and renting the cabin at the beach each August. Action grandparenting also requires allowing family traditions to be challenged and changed as your adult children grow. When my oldest son had his first children, he wanted to be at his own house, with his new family on Christmas morning. My wife and I negotiated with him a new Christmas morning procedure that met his new needs and retained some of our extended family practices. He and his brood now come to our house for a late morning breakfast, thus leaving room for him to do Christmas in his way as well as ours.

Family has two functions. The internal function is the psychosocial protection and nurturing of its members. The external function is accommodation to the culture and the transmission of that culture's ideals.[167] Elders usually have more credibility within their own families than they do in the wider community, so why not begin your eldering there? Action elderhood has great potential as a generative force backing up the parents in the nuclear family. The elder can, in many ways, if he desires, assist in the protection and nurture of the children and grandchildren. The two great social structures, extended family and culture, protect and generate strong elders. Furthermore, they protect human parenting and produce healthy children.

Passing on the Power

The male elder eventually turns over leadership to the younger members of the community. In our culture from age sixty to seventy-five years, we find men withdrawing from power roles such as entrepreneur and politician. In the Far East, the older man is expected to lose interest in temporal affairs and shift toward a more worshipful old age. The oldest cultures perceive the passing of leadership to younger men as the peak of the life cycle.

To elder is to let go of the need for control, coordination and command. Passing on the power is an expression of the wise older man's increasing hunger for connection and simplification of his life. He wants to stir the heart of community while assisting the young in their drive to make the community productive and modern. The elder knows he is not a leader any longer. The leaders are the young whom he has raised. Margaret Mead mused, "There are no elders who know what those who have been reared within the last twenty years know about the world into which they were born." [168] Mead was an elder who believed that former ways of being were precursors rather than models for the leaders of the present.

The generations following the twenty-first century elder will cause and incorporate more and the most rapid changes in our culture than ever. They have watched the locus of world power shift completely away from Cold War status. The means of communication and technology in general have changed enormously in their time. There were no cell phones before 1980. There were only a few computers, and they were large, isolated main frames before 1980. Even the generation Mead studied thirty-five years ago had observed the "definition of humanity, the limits of their explorable universe, the certainties of a known and limited world, the fundamental imperatives of life and death—all change before their eyes."[169] To these experts in change management, the elder relinquishes control.

Model of Good Health

The provider who is the most effective is the healthy man who lives a long life because he is as devoted to his own happiness and physical well being as he is to those whom he loves. Ask a man whom he cares for the most, his wife or himself? It is difficult to find a man who will tell you he must first care for himself to assure he is strong enough to provide for others. This logic escapes Western men who have been taught that they are a tool of society, a "man-o-war" and a machine that moves the cogs of business and industry. They become too busy to care for themselves. If you are an elder who has lived a long life, your model is needed.

American men over sixty-five commit suicide over five times more often than women in their age group. Older men's health is generally worse than older women's. Men are more susceptible to chronic illnesses, including cancer. Men over sixty-five are twice as likely to become victims of violent crime as women. They are four times more likely to become hospitalized for alcohol-related problems.[170] The lamentable facts about men's health show the extent to which our "masculine mystique" has put men in a vulnerable place. As men continue to live shorter, more stressful lives than women, the mystique infuses us with values that discourage men from doing anything to prevent poor health. "Their machine-man view of themselves and their bodies as... productive mechanisms programmed for constant performance and endless labor..."[171] causes them to avoid good health care. Have you a "men's health clinic" in your community? It isn't likely.

The elder is a provider when he influences younger men to take responsibility for their health. Young men need to see the elder doing regular exercise, getting an annual physical and visiting the dentist regularly. The elder needs to model eating a balanced diet, monitoring his cholesterol and replacing processed foods with fruits and vegetables. In this way the elder provides a model of a man who accepts his mortality. Men have a fear of obsolescence and a depleted body rings the "discard" bell. Depletion is not seen simply as an aspect of the second half of life but rather as the end to our usefulness. The elder has a healthy and invigorating image of what an older man can be. He doesn't buy the masculine mystique or the biases about aging in America. He provides hope for younger men about both mature masculinity and the credibility of a balanced older man.

PROTECTOR

The mature masculine expression of protector is not as much a hero as he is a balance of warrior, magician, king and lover. Although heroes are courageous, in Western tradition they have been emotionally mute and invulnerable. They lack transparency and are solitary people. The mature elder balances aspects of the four masculine archetypes in his expression of the role of protector. From warrior energy he expresses a commitment to a cause larger than himself that serves others he admires. From magician energy he gains healer power utilizing insight and reflection to assess the needs of others. From lover energy he finds passion and connection through feeling. From king energy he gets a hunger to affirm others and to restore order from social chaos.

Up through the twentieth century, we raised our sons to believe that a protector must take hazardous risks and accept challenges that could cause him physical and emotional injury. Being courageous often meant denying his fear and plunging into high-risk situations to prove himself. The twenty-first century man protects by being a model of stewardship for men and the earth. He models advocacy for people without hope and perpetuates nondiscrimination. You will find him involved in social action including both volunteer work and political activity. He models nonviolence in his careful use of media, especially television. He protects by leaving a legacy of hope for younger generations. His legacy is a demonstration that the second half of life is for growth, transformation, healing and service. He beseeches his Supreme Being to use him as a vessel for the blessing of the children.

Stewardship

Magician energy fosters harmony with nature. When you balance this with the ordering inclination of the king, the assertiveness of the warrior and the awareness of the Oneness of all things that comes from the lover, you have *stewardship*. The steward is the keeper, entrusted with the affairs of others for whom he is the advocate. You will recall in chapter three how indigenous cultures almost universally assume human beings are responsible for sustaining harmony in nature. The elders who were most respected by primitive people were those who understood the orderly and harmonious whole of the universe. Older people are usually more interested in conservation than are the young. They remember "woods" near your home in which you could play.

How does the elder turn his concern for the earth into stewardship? Let's take a walk once again through the community and watch what the Action Elder does. We find him near his home returning from a walk with a flattened beer can in his hand. He found it on the road, and he

177

knew he would contribute to the beauty of our surroundings by recycling it. Next, we find him calling the local curbside recycling company. He discovers that they will accept not only newspapers, but also the tons of junk mail he used to throw into the garbage can. He tells his neighbors about the news, and they spread the word.

Once again, action elderhood does not require a time-consuming volunteer commitment. There are small behaviors that provide a service while at the same time model advocacy for people and the earth. Action elderhood is living the role of steward as naturally and spontaneously as possible. There are certainly much larger steps a steward of the earth can take, such as gardening and supporting conservationist organizations. My focus here is to affirm life as regularly as possible in the simplest ways at first and then watch and see where it takes you. When the elder behaves this way, he models hope that the ecological destruction we have witnessed in our lifetime can be balanced, at least a little, right within our community. What the action elder creates by this behavior is sacred. Religious, political and scientific leaders from eighty-three nations met a few years ago and declared:

> As scientists many of us have had profound experiences of awe and reverence before the universe. We understood that what is regarded as sacred is more likely to be treated with care and respect. Our planetary home should be so regarded. Efforts to safeguard and cherish the environment need to be infused with a vision of the sacred.[172]

In his day-to-day life, the elder shows care for his family and community as well as the larger community of living organisms with whom he shares the Earth.

A Soul-Nourishing Pace

Another way the elder protects us is by demonstrating ways in which the life- giving breath, or soul, can be nourished. This is the purpose of his spiritual journey. The soul in man is potential until it is actualized in human ways that reflect a man's awe of creation, the love of others, gratitude and the celebration called "harvesting." There are simple yet effective ways that an elder can model soul nourishment.

In this fast-moving culture, we have taken for granted a number of behaviors that starve the soul. One of the most common is watching television and going to movie theaters indiscriminately. At the elder's house, the young will find evidence of discernment in what they will watch on television. Our willingness to indulge in violence and exploitation in entertainment media is one price we pay for haste. The elder has slowed his pace and searches the television for messages of joy, reflection and commitment that are worth viewing. The elder's grandchildren aren't allowed to play violent video games in the elder's home even if the parents allow them to do so in theirs. The children find a warmth and fun-loving spirit in the elder's home that makes up for the restrictions. They are able to consider an alternative approach to the use of media.

As the elder walks his contemplative pace in the community, he extends the boundary of sacred space. My youngest son worked in a fast food restaurant at the counter, serving customers. At age sixteen he was already aware that rude and aggressive customers acted the way they did because of the pressure of time. "Fast food" is a ubiquitous option in culinary pursuit in our culture despite the unhealthy nature of it. We rush in, hardly notice the young human beings working for low wages, grumble an order, complain in a way that does not show common sense, then rush to eat in our automobiles with one hand and take cellular phone calls with the other. My son said it was an uncommon delight when a customer with patient a smile made it clear that their priority was the connection they made with him. The elder models the opposite and compatible response to customer service that I call *customer receptivity.* The core of customer receptivity is the recognition by the customer that the person serving him also wants to be seen. Customer receptivity is modeled by the elder as he waits patiently to be served, focused first on the person serving him and second on the service he is buying. The elder knows that errors made in the customer service process are only expressions of the human journey that are to be expected and honored with patience and generosity.

The elder nourishes us by truly seeing us as we go about performing our work. He accomplishes these things by discovering the pace of life that fits him. He shows us how we can nourish our own soul if only we could take the time to smell the roses. In the 1930s, when Hans Selye outlined the first major theory of stress management, he taught that humans have a limited amount of *adaptability energy*. We have a pool of energy unique to each of us. The effective stress manager learns his capacity and develops practices that allow him to live within that pool. If you don't honor your pool of energy and overuse it, you age too quickly because some of the energy you burn up is not replenishable.

Measuring our pace is a practice that allows us to remain within our pool of adaptability energy. Watch the elder. He harvests his life in part by living within his pool of energy, by understanding the limits of his knowledge and by not exposing himself to stressors that over-tax his emotional life. Then, "A natural unfoldment takes place…which signals a certain time when the accumulated wisdom of a lifetime reaches the state of overflow. Awakened to elderhood, we pour the distillate of our lives into other vessels, an act that not only seeds the future, but that crowns our lives with worth and nobility."[173] He does this not only for his own sake, but also because of his generative concern for the welfare of those who might consider him a mentor, and as a model to younger generations.

Protecting Through Blessing

The unfolding of wisdom, the pouring of the distillate of our lives into younger vessels is both a form of blessing and a *transmission*. By the time my second grandchild was born, I felt a need rise in me to bless her on behalf of the older people in the family. I felt the opportunity and the obligation of grandfatherhood. It was vague, but I believe I was standing in as the representative of my ancestors. I had an opportunity to pass the family name on to my granddaughter, tell her the stories of our generation and share stories about the time before my lifetime. In these ways I transmit a blessing from the ancestors. To accomplish all of this, I needed to bring focus to my granddaughter by creating a ritual of initiation that endorsed her as the newest member of the family.

You will recall how, when we reviewed the belief system of older cultures in chapter three, many believed that in the second half of life you begin to connect metaphysically with your ancestors. This is one reason why older people are shown such deference in China, for example. Older men who have pulled back from leadership of society are inclined to move forward to the "spiritual perimeter [of the culture], to confront the powerful and empowering gods. Older men discover in the supernaturals the strength that they no longer find within themselves…they use prayer…to beseech for themselves and for the people, their fire from the gods."[174] These "gods" include ancestors who now dwell with God. When my granddaughter came into the world, she was very close to God and "the gods," having recently come from within their midst. As I connected to her in the brief ceremony, I was completing a circle: you come from the universe into this life carrying with you the knowledge of your godliness; then you grow, forgetting your source and seek the meaning of your existence; then in the second half of life you begin approaching death, the end of life, and become once again the connection to all who came before and will ever be.

Now I seek out opportunities to be a "transmitter" and source of blessing in the family. Holiday meals are good opportunities to utilize elder energies of blessing. The blessing ceremonies my wife and I sponsored for my children are now models my children may emulate. I plan to attend the baptisms, bar mitzvah and any religious ceremonies honoring my grandchildren to boost the ritual with grandfather energy. My granddaughter's ceremony was simple to create. My wife and I went to my granddaughter's home, and with her parents' permission I did three things with my wife's assistance:

1. I spoke to my granddaughter, who was one week old, about our appreciation for her existence in our life. I affirmed in front of my son and daughter-in-law my vision of the baby's future using words like healthy, successful and happy.

2. I anointed her forehead with a consecrated olive oil a friend had brought to me from Israel. As I touched the baby, I made a verbal commitment to her that I would help her realize her future and her dream.

3. My wife and I gave her a small cross on a chain that her mother will keep for her to wear when she is old enough.

I really didn't know anything about formal blessings as I put together the ceremony, and I felt a little silly doing it. The endorsement I got from my son's eyes, however, made it all seem right. How can a grandfather fail in blessing if he is in love with his grandchild? From chapter one you will recall that a blessing has five parts:

1. Touch

2. Special words

3. An expression of appreciation for the blessed

4. A reference for the blessed of a dream or special future

5. An active commitment to the blessed to help them realize their dream

The blessing is a divination that the blessed need not either accept or understand. It is the elder's declaration before his community, in sacred space, of commitment to the blessed. My granddaughter may never be told that she received this blessing. I believe, nevertheless, that the affirmation in the blessing experience moves the energy of the universe to bring support and vigor to the blessed. The aged were heroes in most ancient societies. Their special stature had to do with their privileged access to the supernatural. Whether you believe the idea of blessing, elders carry a responsibility to both transmit information to the young and to stand ready to serve them as they venture on their journey. If not through blessing, the elder must find a way to assure the young that he is available and passionate about their success.

Heed Those Without Hope

The creation of sacred space begins when one person is seen by another. The homeless, unemployed, disabled and other victims of our prejudice can begin a move up and out of economic and mental poverty if more of us were willing to see them. The elder, moving with thanatos energy, sees the homeless. The elder sees them much like he sees himself: They were born to a mother in a place called home and had a father or longed for one. Like himself, they are spirits, splinters of God, and that ties them together. Like him, they need to be seen. The ruin of a nation begins in the homes. Many hopeless men would add that the ruin of homes begins in the heart of the father. Remembering the statistics about fatherlessness and that nearly one-third of children are born out of wedlock in the USA, the elder shivers at what the statistic must be for the poor, the homeless and minorities.

Black activist and scholar W.E.B. DuBois wrote in 1912, "Ought children be born to us? Have we a right to make human souls face what we face today? The answer is clear: if the great battle of human rights against poverty, against color prejudice is to be won, it must be won not in our day, but in the day of our children's children."[175] The elder knows he must depend on the next generation to do the next great work in society. Like DuBois, the elder expects to be supportive to the social activists among the young and knows his responsibility is to hold the container for them, rather than lead "the great battle of human rights" himself.

How does the elder hold the container for the advocates of the hopeless? Let's take it in levels of intensity of involvement. At the First Level of action elderhood the elder *sees* the homeless or the victim of discrimination. They know they are seen because in First Level action the hopeless hear the elder say, "May I help you?" or "Do you know of a place you can sleep tonight?" because he knows how to find shelters in his city. Driving in a suburban area recently I saw a man walking in the rain with no shoes or hat. I was in a hurry and continued on so that I would be on time for something I thought was more important. I didn't even express First Level action because I didn't take the opportunity for involvement.

At Level Two action, the elder might have done this instead: Once he saw the man he would stop his car at the next public phone and call whomever was expecting him to report that he would be a little late for his appointment. He would then have taken his umbrella, left his car, crossed the street and walked to where the shoeless man was standing. "Pardon me, I see that you have no shoes. Would you allow me to help you find a pair?" From this point forward, it would be the shoeless man's right to respond any way that he wished. If he accepts the offer, the two men could arrange to meet somewhere safe for both after the elder finds some shoes that will fit the man. The elder needn't take big risks like giving the man a ride in his car or inviting him into his home. The act of approaching the man connects the two at the heart and builds sacred space.

Level Three actions on behalf of the hopeless would include offering elder wisdom about the organizations that seek to improve the lives of unemployed, minority, disabled, imprisoned and homeless men. You will find that the United Way, churches and charitable organizations need mature impassioned people as advisors and sources of leadership. Most of these groups are governed by boards of volunteer directors made up of people who are just folks like you and I. You need nothing but time and interest to qualify. By the management and advocacy of these directors, organizations are funded that employ DuBois's children's children, who do the Level Four work in the trenches. DuBois went on to say that the reason our children are on the frontline is that the elders have on them the "blood and dust of battle," and the young, "theirs the rewards of victory" won in our early efforts to free the hopeless. "If they are not there [doing our Level Four work], because we have not brought them to the world, then we have been the guiltiest factor in conquering ourselves."[176]

Level Four

Don't let me discourage you from Level Four action if you desire it. I want to inspire you to consider yourself a natural resource. It is possible to be a natural resource and to actualize in small ways. North Americans, more than most peoples believe in the potential of what one person can do. If we start with a smile, an extended moment of accessibility, or a gift of a pair of shoes, then anyone can play a part in action elderhood.

We all admire elders who have excelled at Level Four action. Nelson Mandella, Jimmy Carter, Benjamin Spock and others have modeled Level Four action at an older age than most activists. If you are ready, you can sit with dying AIDS patients in a hospice, build dikes against flooding rivers, counsel boys in gangs on the street, mentor drug abusers in a drop-in center, tutor children with reading problems, deliver food to the poor, and do hands-on political campaigning. The balanced elder integrates the reflective energy of thanatos with the creative energy of libido. Libido still drives us in the second half of life—for some it remains at a high level throughout life. The wonderful reality about the sage is that we can all depend on him to make good judgements about how to use his energy.

TEACHER

Men and women share the role of teacher of cultural tradition. The masculine viewpoint of folklore and beliefs was for most of history influenced by the man's roles of protector and provider. Up until the Industrial Revolution, men taught the young how to survive and, as an extension of that, how to protect his family. This included teaching crafts, skills with tools and skills with weapons. In the eighteenth century, with the advent of public school systems, men were teachers of knowledge, comportment and the governing of the community. In the nineteenth century men modeled how to work for a wage in addition to working to create products of living and trade. They taught how to build and maintain corporations. In the twentieth century men coach, guide and model with a greater feminine influence. The evolution of man has brought with it an increasing influence of the feminine in men and the masculine in women.

The elder of the twenty-first century seeds the future in his teaching role. He is a mentor, storyteller and wisdomkeeper who stands ready to serve the young people who seek him out. He models "following your own bliss" while at the same time seeking out young people to assure the success of their journey. The modern elder-teacher models a life of soundness and models a morality, risking that he may even appear old-fashioned. He rejects living in a way that sanctifies the destructive masculine mystique.

Wisdomkeeper

The elder in older societies was obligated by tradition to pass on his knowledge of the community's history. It mattered little how balanced the older people were when it came to passing on *oral tradition*: the telling of stories only available in verbal form because the written word was not utilized for this purpose or didn't exist. Even a frustrated and angry man could tell his version of community stories. The more balanced and heart-centered a man is, however, the greater is his desire to share because of his passion for the success of the young. This man is a *wisdomkeeper.*

> *When October winds do blow,*
> *Then a man his wheat must sow.*
> *Thus must act a man of worth*
> *Who has arrived at sixty years:*
> *He must sow in young folk's ears*
> *Wisdom all their hearts to fill,*
> *And give them charity if he will*[177]

Watch the elder wisdomkeeper at a recent family gathering. He asks the family to gather in one room. Once they are all settled, the elder announces that he has a tape recorder going and that he wants each person to tell their favorite family story. Throughout the next hour, ten vignettes about the elder's family are recorded. The elder told a story as well. Through this ritual, which he sponsored, the family's wisdomkeeper not only created a place to tell his version of family history, but also facilitated a family process that added considerably to the store of family history he supervises. He offered to tell more stories at the Fourth-of-July picnic where the family traditionally gathers.

My mother-in-law, who is eighty years old, is writing the story of her life. She occasionally asks several of us to read it and offer her feedback. In this manner, she not only tunes up the content of her book, but also gives the family an excuse to discuss family history with her. She stimulated me to contact my father and ask him to do the same. He "bah, humbugged" the idea but I convinced him to talk to a tape recorder. He still uses dial telephones, so I wasn't going to risk asking him to talk to a video recorder. I got one tape from him with just one side used. Driven by wisdomkeeper energy, I came back to him with a number of questions about the material on the tape that he could expand on in a second recording. By this method I got the reluctant patriarch to fill two tapes.

In this manner, a man "saves" himself for his children in the same way we save data to the memory of a computer.

One function of the older people in a family should be the linking together of family history and its present members. Being wise is good too, but we aren't always considered wise by the young. Thoreau said when he was thirty years old, "Age is no better, hardly, so well qualified for an instructor as youth for it has not profited so much as it has lost."[178] Thank goodness for Emerson, however, who said "...with the appearance of the wise man the State expires. The appearance of character makes the State unnecessary."[179]

If we look for opportunities to tell the family stories and encourage the maintenance of family history, we take ourselves into the mainstream of the family. The extended family has disintegrated and the nuclear family is splintering into single-parent and blended families, further weakening the ties that bind the generations. The elder visible at the core of his extended family can't repair broken families, but he does model for the children the meeting of life with "spiritual wisdom, grace and courage."[180]

The wisdomkeeper of the twenty-first century has a new look. He does not fit our stereotype of a wrinkled Native American sitting quietly and occasionally uttering words that overwhelm with their depth and appropriateness. Today the wisdomkeeper looks like he has lived a fairly long time, is in pretty good health, and has a passion for seeing people connected. He does everything he can to be the glue that holds the disparate parts of the family and community together.

Reaching Out to Younger Men

To come of age, to come to mature masculinity, a young male needs models. He needs models of both feminine and masculine expression in a man. He needs to see the four masculine archetypes balanced in his mentor's expression. "When we stand physically close to our father, something—something moves over that can't be described in material terms..."[181] And it goes both ways, for a man can't possibly know what life means until he has a child and experiences the love of that child. In fact it is his children's expectations of him that makes a father his best.

The most mature role a man will play is father. If in the chaos of the dysfunctional twenty-first century family, the father continues to withdraw from the family, the modeling must come from some other man.

Take a few minutes and make a list of the people, men and women, who, to any extant, had a positive influence on you. My piano teacher was in my life twice a month. Her sensitive manner and her respect for me caused me to love the piano. My best friend in my senior class in high school once told me he didn't feel I showed adequate respect for a girl I dated. He was my first morality coach. The man who was my first management-consulting customer was the labor relations coordinator for a paper mill. He modeled for me a passion for a quality work life. He was extraordinarily patient with the management of the mill that he needed to confront in ongoing negotiations. Doug, the elder I told you about in chapter one, was obese. He did not model perfection. He was not perfect, but he walked in the world with a love for others that was incomparable. He maintained a calling to the spiritual being in others. It was a kind of summons to the heart of the other.

Some of us are blessed with numerous mentors. All of us were touched by a few. An eighty-year-old man in my church told me he could not recall ever having a mentor. He is an unhappy man, and I suspect he dismissed his own occasional impact as a mentor to others, as well. It is also true that many mentors and mentees don't always know that mentoring is happening. Mentoring is the giving of a blessing to the person for whom you are the advocate.

Blessings are given in subtle ways including touch, the use of special words and a look that *sees* the blessed. "Looking back, I realize that I was blessed with mentors at every crucial stage of my young life…But a funny thing happened on the way to full adulthood: the mentors stopped coming. For several years I waited for the next one in vain…"[182] This man realized in the second half of life that it was now time for him to become a mentor.

In our sadness about having an emotionally detached father or a grandfather who died when we were young, we often find ourselves waiting for a guru and deliverance. Admittedly, there are very few models of eldership. The ideals to which I suggest the elder-in-training aspire are high indeed. In the community, action elderhood will begin to meet the need some men have for deliverance. It fills the hole in men left unfilled by male initiation.

A few places where older men and younger men meet are worth mentioning. The scouting programs in North America not only connect men and boys, but also offer rites of passage. The increasingly demanding challenge of moving higher and higher in the ranks of scouting is an initiation into manhood. The Service Corps of Retired Executives, SCORE, provides free advice to young business people. Over 13,000 retired business managers, entrepreneurs and professionals, who are mostly men, donate almost unlimited time to the task of advising on the manner in which you form a new business. The Small Business Administration of the US Government sponsors the program. The Big Brothers, one of America's oldest and largest mentoring programs, can't find enough qualified men who will volunteer. Studies have shown that boys with mentors in Big Brothers are 46 percent less likely to begin using drugs and 52 percent are less likely to skip school.

All of these programs need more participation from men. The biggest demand for action elderhood, however, is inside your personal sphere of influence—family, community, church and workplace. It is likely that most of the people inside your sphere will not expect action elderhood from you. That is why I suggest that the aspiring elder move into action in small ways at first, gradually developing the roles of provider, protector and teacher. The process might begin with increasing your accessibility and then moving to some minor community advocacy such as donating blood to the Red Cross or beginning a dialogue with the neighbors you have not gotten to know. No matter how elder-like you presently are in your extended family, this is where you are probably going to find the most opportunity for action elderhood. How much preparation have you made to offer leadership to the young members of your family? Are you trying your best to take care of yourself so that you model the fourfold balance of physical, mental, intellectual and spiritual being? Have you begun to supervise the collection of family historical artifacts?

As you grow in confidence, you will seek ways to initiate your elder role. This requires, you will recall, not only a demonstrated concern with nature but increased movement in the direction of those who need your advocacy and your blessing. Gradually, the family will begin to notice your soul-nourishing pace and lifestyle. "Where is grandpa?" one child will say to another. "Oh, I think he is meditating again," reports the other with both pride and a little embarrassment. You will find that you have an increasing tendency to look out for others, see them and desire to give a little of your time. It doesn't matter whether you behave with Level One, Two, Three or Four action. What matters is that you look increasingly for ways to affirm life. It is this hunger that brings out the wisdomkeeper in a man.

The move away from the *doingness* of our earlier years into the *beingness* of the second half of life does not mean that elders are passive. Being is a calling to the being in others, a resonance with others. Elder being is a state of accessibility and a passion for celebration of long life's experience, service, and an inner intimacy with your eternal spirit. Elder being is an understanding of mortality, the spiritual journey and an earnest concern for the quality of life on this planet. Elder being is a restoration of ancient man's uncontrollable commitment to cultivating and sowing the next generation—*from the heart.*

ENDNOTES

1   Smalley Gary and Trent, John. *Blessing*. Tape cassette. Pocket Books. 1990.

2   Gennep, Arnold Van. *The Rites of Passage*. University of Chicago Press, Chicago. 1960. Translation of Gennep's 1908, Les rites de passage. p. 50.

3   Gilbran Kahlil. *The Prophet*. New York. Alfred A. Knopf. 1951. p.18.

4   Campbell, Joseph. *Myths to Live By*. Bantam Books. New York. 1972. p. 46.

5   Chinen, Allan. *In The Ever After*. Chiron Publ. Wilmette, Illinois. 1989. p. 150-151.

6   Schachter – Shalomi, Zalman. *Ageing and Sageing*. Warner Books. NY. 1995. p. 16-17.

7   Chinen, *In The Ever After*. p. 152.

8   Erickson, Eric. *Vital Involvement In Old Age*. W.W. Norton & Co. New York. 1986. p. 37-38.

9   Demos, John. *Past, Present and Personal: The Family and Life Course in American History*. Oxford University Press. NY. 1986. p. 5.

10 Gutmann, David. *Reclaimed Powers*. Northwestern University Press. Evanston, III. p. 1994.

11 Kauth, Bill. *A Circle of Men*. St. Martin's Press. New York. 1992. p. 118.

12   Schachter – Shalomi, p. 83.

13   Gibran, p. 71.

14   Larue, Gerald A. *Gero-Ethics*. Prometheus Books. 1992. p. 39.

15   Archenbaum, W. Andrews. *"The Aging of the First New Nation"* In Alan Pfizer and Lydia Bronte, Eds. Our Aging Society. WW Norton Co. NY. 1986. p. 20.

16   Mathews, Mitford M. *A Dictionary of Americanism on Historical Principles*. University of Chicago Press, Chicago. 1951. Vol. 2. p. 1793.

17   Turner, Frederick G. *"Middle Western Pioneer Democracy."* (1918) in The Frontier in American History. Rinehart and Winston. 1962. New York. p. 339.

18   Demos. p. 143

19   Fischer, David H. *Growing Old in America*. Oxford University Press. NY. 1978. p. 68.

20   *Ibid.*

21   Fischer, p. 39.

22   Kimbrell, Andrew. *The Masculine Mystique*. Ballantine Books. NY. 1995. p. 35.

23   Demos. p. 174.

24   Gurdjieff, G.I. *Meetings With Remarkable Men*. New York: E.P. Dutton. 1969. p. 36.

25   Fischer. p. 79.

26   Polanyi, Karl. *The Great Transformation*. Beacon Press. Boston. 1957. p. 270

27   Kimbrell, p. 39.

28   Goldberg, Herb. *The Hazards of Being Male*. New American Library. NY. 1976. p. 92.

29   Heard, Gerald. *The Five Ages of Man*. The Julian Press. New York. 1963. p. 258.

30   de Beauvoir, Simone. *The Coming of Age*. GP Putnam's Sons. New York. 1972. p. 50

31   Heard. p. 259.

32   Chinen, p. 146-148.

33   Levinson, Daniel J. *The Seasons of a Man's Life*. Ballantine Books. NY. 1978. p. 91.

34   *Ibid.*, p. 100.

35   Hesse, Hermann. *Siddartha*. New Directions. New York. 1951. p. 106.

36   Buber, Martin. *"The Disciple"* in *A Believing Humanism*. Simon and Schuster. NY. 1967. p. 41.

37   Demos, p. 44.

38   Gutmann, p. 91.

39   Schacter – Shalomi. p. 5.

40   *Ibid.* p. 13-14.

41   Zukav, Gary. *The Seat of the Soul*. Simon and Schuster. New York. 1989. p. 186.

42   *Ibid.* p. 31.

43   Kimbrell, Andrew. *Masculine Mystique*. New York. Ballantine Books. 1995. p. 48.

44   Demos, John. *Past, Present and Personal: The Family and Life Course in American History*. New York: Oxford University Press. 1986. p. 54.

45   Schor, Juliet B. *The Overworked American*. Harper Collins. New York. 1992. p. 45.

46   Wells, H.G. *The Outline of History*. vol. II. Garden City Books. New York. 1920. p. 656.

47 Farrell, Warren. *The Myth of Male Power.* Simon and Schuster. NY. 1993. p. 30.

48 *Ibid.* p. 31.

49 Kimbrell, p. 5.

50 Farrell, p. 33.

51 Poponoe, David. *Life Without Fathers.* The Free Press. NY. 1996. p. 31.

52 Levant, Ronald F. "The New Psychology of Men." *Professional Psychology Research Practice.* 1996. vol. 27. No. 3. pp. 259-265.

53 Fox, Matthew. *The Coming of the Cosmic Christ.* Harper and Row. San Francisco. 1988. Quoting Philosopher Gabriel Marcel. p. 163.

54 Moore, Robert and Gillette, Douglas. *King, Warrior, Magician, Lover.* Harper Collins Pub. San Francisco. 1990. p. 90.

55 *Ibid.*

56 Kimbrell, p. 46.

57 *Ibid.,* p. 49.

58 Farrell, p. 50.

59 John Laffin. *Brassey's Battles: 3500 Years of Conflict, Campaigns and Wars From A to Z.* London: A Wheaton and Co. 1986. p. 399.

60 Goldberg, p. 105.

61 Kimbrell, p. 74.

62 Silverstein, Olga and Beth Rashbaum. *The Courage to Raise Good Men.* Penguin Books. NY. 1994. p. 30.

63 Kimura, Doreen. *"Sex Difference in the Brain."* Scientific American. September, 1992 p. 119-125. Anne Moir and David Jessel. "Brain Sex" *Behavioral Endocrinology.* Cambridge, MA: MIT Press/Bradford Books. 1992.

64 Popenoe, p. 184.

65   Elizabeth Fenner. *"Sizing Up the Risks of Living Together" Money.* July, 1995. p. 96-97.

66   Modell, John, Fran F. Furstenberg Jr. and Douglas Strong. *"The Timing of Marriage In The Transition to Adulthood: Continuity and Change, 1869-1975" American Journal of Sociology.* 1978. vol. 4, p. S120-S150.

67   Fenner, *Money,* p. 96.

68   U.S. Bureau of the Census. Current Population Reports. Series P-20. No. 467. (Wash. DC US Government Printing Office. April, 1993) XVI.

69   Popenoe, p. 36.

70   Furstenberg, Frank and Christine W. Nord. *"Parenting Apart: Patterns of Childbearing After Marital Disruption." Journal of Marriage and the Family.* 1985. 47(4): p. 893-905.

71   Advance Report of the Final Mortality Statistics, 1991. vol. 42. No. 3, Supplement, Monthly Vital Statistics Report. (Hyattsville, Md.: U.S. Dept. of Health and Human Services. Sept. 9, 1993.9, 30.

72   de Lisser, Eleena. *"For Inner-City Youth a Hard Life May Lead To a Hard Sentence." Wall Street Journal.* Nov. 30, 1993. p. 1.

73   National Commission on Children. *Beyond Rhetoric.* Douglas J. Besharov, testimony before the Select Committee on Children, Youth and Families. (Washington D.C. US Government Printing Office. 1987. p. 32-33).

74   Parke, Ross D. *Fathers.* Cambridge: Harvard University Press. 1981. p. 2.

75   E. Anthony Rotundo. "American Fatherhood: A Historical Perspective." *American Behavioral Scientist.* vol. 29. No. 1. (Sept./ Oct. 1985): p. 7-25.

76   Popenoe, p. 12.

77   Demos, p. 55.

78 *Ibid.* p. 49-50.

79 Popenoe, p. 158.

80 Mead, Margaret. *Male and Female.* New York. 1955. p. 55.

81 Malinowski, Bronislaw. *Sex, Culture and Myth.* New York: Harcourt, Brace and World. 1962. p. 63.

82 Gutmann, David. *Reclaimed Powers.* Northwestern University Press. Evanston, Illinois. 1987. p. 226.

83 Heard, Gerald. *The Five Ages of Man.* The Julian Press. New York. 1963. pp. 164-165.

84 de Beauvoir. *Old Age.* Harmondsworth. New York. 1977. p. 96.

85 Fischer, *Growing Old in America.* p. 6.

86 Gurdjieff, G.I. *Meetings With Remarkable Men.* E.P. Dutton. New York. 1974. p. 36.

87 Cook, Shelburne. "Aging of and in Populations." P.S. Timiras, Editor. *Developmental Physiology and Aging.* New York. 1972. p. 595.

88 Simmons, Leo. *The Role of the Aged in Primitive Society.* New Haven. 1945. p. 17.

89 Fischer, *Growing Old in America.* p. 10.

90 Leslie, Gerald R. and Sheila K. Korman. *The Family in Social Context.* Oxford University Press. New York, 1989. p. 87.

91 Dewey, J. and J.H. Tufts. *Ethics.* New York. 1913. p. 17-18.

92 In his book, *Wisdom of the Elders*, biologist David Suzuki and his co-author, Peter Knudtson, expand the concept of *eldering* so that they find both indigenous people and modern day scientists qualify as *elders*. Much of the next few pages is a paraphrase of key parts of their book. New York. Bantam Books. 1992.

93 Van Gennep, Arnold. *The Rites of Passage.* Chicago. University of Chicago Press. 1960. p. 109.

94 Suzuki, *Wisdom.* p. 230.

95   *Ibid.* p. 16-18.

96   *Ibid.*

97   Miller, Alice. *The Untouched Key: Tracing Childhood Trauma in Creativity and Destructiveness.* New York: Doubleday. 1990. p. 155, 158.

98   Fischer, David H. *Growing Old in America.* New York. 1978. p. 17.

99   France, Peter. *Hermits.* St. Martin's Press. New York. 1996. p. 5.

100 France, *Hermits.* p. 6.

101 Xenophon, "Memorabilia of Socrates," in *Socratic Discourse Plato and Xenophon.* Everyman's Library, London. 1910. p. 32.

102 France, *Hermits.* p. 10.

103 St. Jerome. *Letters.* p. 61. Letter XIV. Quoted in George Minois. *History of Old Age.* University of Chicago Press. 1987. p. 130.

104 Aristotle. *The Ethics.* Trans. J.A.K. Thomson. Harmondsworth. 1959. IV.I; VIII. p. 3-6.

105 Plutarch. "Whether an old man should engage in public affairs?" *Moralia.* X. "Old men in public affairs." 784. p. 81. Quoted in Minois. *History of Old Age.* p. 73.

106 *Ibid.* p. 75.

107 Marcel, Gabriel. *The Decline of Wisdom.* Philosophical Library. New York. 1955. p. 40.

108 Rinpoche, p. 153.g

109 Minois, George. p. 118.

110 Marcel, Gabriel. *The Decline of Wisdom.* Philosophical Library. New York. 1955. p. 42.

111 *Ibid.* p. 43.

112 Fischer, David H. *Growing Old in America.* Oxford University Press, New York. 1978. p. 16.

113 Shakespeare, William. "As You Like It." In *The Annotated Shakespeare*. Vol. I. The Comedies. Editor, A.L. Rouse. Longmeadow Press. 1928. p. 360.

114 Erasmus. *Praise of Folly.* Trans. Betty Radice. London. 1974. Cap. 13, 37.

115 Wells, H.G. *The Outline of History*. Vol. II. Garden City, New York. 1920. p. 588.

116 Donne, John. "Death's Duell or, a Consolation to the Soule, Against the Dying Life, and Living Death of the Body." *In The Complete Poetry and Selected Prose of John Doone.* Editor: Charles M. Coffin. New York. Random House. 1952. 58 ff.

117 Kimbrell, *The Masculine Mystique*. p. 30.

118 Hammond, J.L. and Barbara. *The Village Laborer, 1760-1832*. London: Longmans Green. 1912. p. 10. Quoted in Kimbrell, p. 54.

119 Marcel, Gabriel. *The Decline of Wisdom*. Philosophical Library. New York. 1955. p. 46-47.

120 Gutmann, p. 217.

121 Taylor, A.E. *Socrates.* Doubleday: Garden City, N.Y. 1953. p. 149.

122 Buber, Martin. "To Hallow This Life." Harper and Brothers Pub: NY. 1958. p. 87.

123 Popenoe, David. *Life Without Fathers*. New York. The Free Press. 1996. p. 111.

124 Farrell, Warren. *The Myth of Male Power*. Simon and Schuster: NY. 1993. p. 17.

125 Myss, Caroline. *Anatomy of the Spirit.* New York. Harmony Books. 1996. p. 185-186.

126 Chinen, Alan B. *In the Ever After*. Chiron Pub: Wilmette, ILL. 1994. p. 149.

127 Fox, Robin. *Encounter With Anthopology*. Peregrine: London. 1975. p. 122.

128 Whitmont, E.C. *The Symbolic Quest*. Barrie and Rockliff: London. 1969.

129 *Ibid.* p. 182.

130 Moore, Robert and Douglas Gillette. *King, Warrior, Magician, Lover: Rediscovering the Archetypes of the Mature Masculine*. Harper: San Francisco. 1990. p. 15.

131 *Ibid.* p. 13.

132 Whitmont, p. 178.

133 Eliade, Mircea. *The Sacred and the Profane: The Nature of Religion: The Significance of Religious Myth, Symbolism and Ritual Within Life and Culture*. New York: Harcourt Brace Jovanovich, 1959. p. 63.

134 Whitmont, p. 182.

135 Moore and Gillette. p. 121.

136 Gibran, Kahlil. *The Prophet*. Alfred A. Knopf, New York. p. 13.

137 Moore, Robert and Douglas Gillette. *The Magician Within*. Harper. San Francisco. 1993. p. 111.

138 Erickson, Erik. *Childhood and Society*. W.W. Norton and Co. New York. 1950. p. 269.

139 Bly, Robert. *Iron John*. Vintage Books. New York. 1990. p. 221.

140 Arrien, Angeles. *The Second Half of Life*. "Sounds True" tape series. Boulder, Colo. 1998.

141 Moore, Robert and Douglas Gillette. *The Magician Within*. William Morrow and Co. Inc. New York. 1993. p. 202.

142 Eliade, M. *Rites and Symbols of Initiation*. New York. Harper and Row. 1958. P. 132.

143 Van Gennep, Arnold. *The Rites of Passage*. Chicago. The University of Chicago Press. 1960. p. 2.

144 Bunzel, Ruth. "Introduction to Zuni Ceremonialism." *44th Annual Report of the Bureau of American Ethnology.* Wash. D.C. 1932. p. 516-17

145 Van Gennep. *Rites.* pp. 82-83.

146 Foster, Steven and Meredith Little. *The Book of the Vision Quest.* Fireside. New York. 1992. pp. 21-25.

147 Foster, Steven and Meredith Little. *The Trail to the Sacred Mountain.* Lost Borders Press. 1984. p.53.

148 Dychtwald, Ken. *Age Wave.* Bantam Books. New York. 1990. p. 38.

149 Augustine. "Enarrationes in Psalmos. 112.2 in Erich Przywara, Editor. *An Augustine Synthesis.* Steed and Ward. New York. 1945.

150 Suzuki, David and Peter Knudtson. *Wisdom of the Elders.* Bantam. New York. 1992. p. 225.

151 Butler, Robert M., M.D. "Successful Aging and the Role of Life Review" *Journal of the American Geriatrics Society.* vol. XXII. Dec. 1974. No. 12. p. 534.

152 Levinson, Daniel. *The Seasons of a Man's Life.* Ballantine Books. New York. 1978. p. 224.

153 Bianchi, Eugene. *Aging as a Spiritual Journey.* Crossword. New York. 1982. p. 65.

154 Iser, Lynne, compiler. *The Spiritual Eldering Workbook.* Spiritual Eldering Institute. 1996. p. 52-53.

155 Bianchi, p. 181.

156 Albom, Mitch. *Tuesdays With Morrie.* Doubleday. New York. 1997. p. 83-84.

157 Iser, p. 5.

158 Gutmann, David. *Reclaimed Powers.* Northwestern University Press. Evanston, III. 1987. p. 253.

159 Fox, Matthem. *The Coming of the Cosmic Christ.* Harper and Row Pub. San Francisco. 1988. p. 48.

160 France, Peter. *Hermits.* St. Martin's Press. New York. 1996. p. 48.

161 Campbell, Joseph. *Myths To Live By.* Bantam Books. New York. 1972. p. 36.

162 Pintauro, Joseph and Sister Corita. *To Believe in God.* Harper and Row Pub. New York. 1968. p. 15.

163 Rinpoche, Sogyal. *The Tibetan Book of the Living and Dying.* Harper. San Francisco. 1993. p. 136.

164 Khan, H.I. *The Sufi Message of Hazrat Inayat Khan.* vol. X. Barrie and Jenkins. London. 1964. p. 77.

165 Popenoe, David. *Life Without Father.* The Free Press. New York: 1996. p. 191.

166 Campbell, Angus. *The Sense of Well Being in America.* McGraw-Hill. New York. 1981. p. 231.

167 Minuchin, Salvador. *Families and Family Therapy.* Harvard University Press. Cambridge, Mass. 1974. p. 46.

168 Mead, Margaret. *Culture and Commitment.* Natural History Press. New York. 1970. p. 61.

169 *Ibid.*

170 "Alcohol Problems Prevalent Among Elderly." *Washington Post,* Sept. 8, 1993. p. A5 quoted in Andrew Kimbrell, *The Masculine Mystique.* Ballantine Books. New York. 1995.

171 Kimbrell, p. 210-211.

172 "Preserving and Cherishing the Earth: An Appeal For Joint Commitment in Science and Religion." Moscow. 1991. Quoted in David Suzuki and Peter Knudtson. *Wisdom of the Elders.* Bantam Books. New York. 1992. p. 227.

173 Schacter-Shalomi, Rabbi Zalman. *From Age-ing to Sage-ing.* Warner Books. New York. 1995. p. 190.

174 Guttman, David. *Reclaimed Powers.* Northwestern University Press. Evanston, Illinois. 1994. p. 221.

175 Du Bois, W.E.B. *An ABC of Color.* International Pub. New York. 1964. p. 44.

176 *Ibid.*

177 Grant Kalendrier et compost des bergiers. 1500 edition, quoted by J. Morawski. "Les douze mois figurez" in Archivum Romanicum. 1926. p. 351.

178 Thoreau, Henry David. *Walden.* Signet Classics Edition. 1980. p. 11.

179 Copleston, F. *A History of Philosophy.* 1947. vol, 8. Part II. p. 20.

180 Schachter, p. 220.

181 *A Gathering of Men.* Video interview by Bill Moyers of Robert Bly. 1990.

182 Palmer, Parker. *The Courage to Teach.* Jossey-Bass Inc. Pub. San Francisco. 1998. p. 25.

BIBLIOGRAPHY

Albom, Mitch. *Tuesdays With Morrie*. Doubleday. New York. 1997.

"Alcohol Problems Prevalent Among Elderly." *Washington Post*, Sept. 8, 1993. p. A5 quoted in Andrew Kimbrell, *The Masculine Mystique*. Ballantine Books. New York. 1995.

Archenbaum, W. Andrew. "The Aging of the First New Nation." In Alan Pfizer and Lydia Bronte, Eds. *Our Aging Society*. WW Norton Co. NY. 1986.

Aristotle. *The Ethics*. Trans. J.A.K. Thomson. Harmondsworth. 1959. IV.I; VIII.3-6.

Arrien, Angeles. *The Second Half of Life*. "Sounds True" tape series. Boulder, Colo. 1998.

Augustine *Synthesis*. Steed and Ward. New York. 1945.

de Beauvoir. *Old Age*. Harmondsworth. New York. 1977.

de Beauvoir, Simone. *The Coming of Age*. GP Putnam's Sons. New York. 1972

Bianchi, Eugene. Aging as a Spiritual Journey. Crossword. New York. 1982.

Bly, Robert. *Iron John*. Vintage Books. New York. 1990.

Buber, Martin. "The Disciple" in *A Believing Humanism*. Simon and Schuster. NY. 1967.

Buber, Martin. *To Hallow This Life*. Harper and Brothers Pub: NY. 1958.

Bunzel, Ruth. "Introduction to Zuni Ceremonialism." 44th Annual Report of the Bureau of American Ethnology. Wash. D.C. 1932.

Butler, Robert M., MD. "Successful Aging and the Role of Life Review" in *Journal of the American Geriatrics Society*. vol. XXII. Dec. 1974. No.12. p.534.

Campbell, Angus. *The Sense of Well Being in America*. McGraw-Hill. New York. 1981.

Campbell, Joseph. *Myths to Live By*. Bantam Books. New York. 1970.

Chinen, Allan. *In The Ever After*. Chiron Pub. Wilmette, Illinois. 1989.

Cook, Shelburne. "Aging of and in Populations." P.S. Timiras, Editor, *Developmental Physiology and Aging*. New York. 1972. p.595.

Copleston, F. A *History of Philosophy*. 1947. Vol, 8. Part II.

Demos, John. *Past, Present and Personal: The Family and Life Course in American History*. Oxford University Press. NY 1986.

Dewey, J. and J.H. Tufts. *Ethics*. New York. 1913.

Donne, John. "Death's Duell or, a Consolation to the Soule, Against the Dying Life, and Living Death of the Body." *The Complete Poetry and Selected Prose of John Do*one. Editor: Charles M. Coffin. New York. Random House. 1952.

Du Bois, W.E.B. *An ABC of Color*. International Pub. New York. 1964.

Dychtwald, Ken. *Age Wave*. Bantam Books. New York. 1990.

E. Anthony Rotundo. "American Fatherhood: A Historical Perspective."

American Behavioral Scientist. vol. 29. No.1. (Sept./Oct. 1985): pp. 7-25.

Eliade, M. Rites and Symbols of Initiation. New York. Harper and Row. 1958.

Eliade, Mircea. *The Sacred and the Profane: The Nature of Religion: The Significance of Religious Myth, Symbolism and Ritual Within Life and Culture*. New York: Harcourt Brace Jovanovich, 1959

Erasmus. *Praise of Folly*. Trans. Betty Radice. London. 1974.

Erikson, Erik. *Childhood and Society*. W.W. Norton and Co. New York. 1950.

Erikson, Eric. *Vital Involvement in Old Age*. W.W. Norton & Co. New York. 1986.

Farrell, Warren. *The Myth of Male Power*. Simon and Schuster. NY. 1993.

Fenner, Elizabeth. "Sizing Up The Risks of Living Together" in *Money*. July, 1995.

Fischer, David H. *Growing Old in America*. Oxford University Press. N.Y.1978.

Foster, Steven and Meredith Little. *The Book of the Vision Quest*. Fireside. New York. 1992.

Foster, Steven and Meredith Little. *The Trail to the Sacred Mountain*. Lost Borders Press. 1984.

Fox, Matthew. *The Coming of the Cosmic Christ*. Harper and Row. San Francisco. 1988

Quoting philosopher Gabriel Marcel.

Fox, Robin. *Encounter With Anthropology*. Peregrine: London. 1975.

France, Peter. *Hermits*. St. Martin's Press. New York. 1996.

Furstenberg, Frank and Christine W. Nord. "Parenting Apart: Patterns of Childbearing After Marital Disruption." *In Journal of Marriage and the Family*. 1985. 47(4): pp. 893-905.

A Gathering of Men.Video interview by Bill Moyers of Robert Bly. 1990

Gibran, Kahlil. *The Prophet*. Alfred A. Knopf. New York 1951.

Goldberg, Herb. *The Hazards of Being Male*. New American Library. NY. 1976.

Grant Kalendrier et compost des bergiers. 1500 edition, quoted by J. Morawski. "Les douze mois figurez" in Archivum Romanicum. 1926.

Gurdjieff, G.I. *Meetings With Remarkable Men*. New York: E.P. Dutton.1969.

Gutmann, David. *Reclaimed Powers*. Northwestern University Press. Evanston, Ill.1994.

Hammond, J.L. and Barbara. *The Village Lab*orer, 1760-1832. London: Longmans Green. 1912. p. 10 Quoted in Kimbrell, p.54.

Heard, Gerald. *The Five Ages of Man*. The Julian Press. New York. 1963.

Hesse, Hermann. *Siddartha*. New Directions. New York. 1951.

Iser, Lynne, Compiler. *The Spiritual Eldering Workbook*. Spiritual Eldering Institute. 1996.

Kauth, Bill. *A Circle of Men*. St. Martin's Press. New York. 1992.

Khan, H.I. *The Sufi Message of Hazrat Inayat Kha*n. vol. X. Barrie and Jenkins. London. 1964.

Kimbrell, Andrew. *The Masculine Mystique*. Ballantine Books. NY 1995.

Kimura, Doreen. "Sex Difference in the Brain." *Scientific American*. September, 1992: pp. 119-125. Anne Moir and David Jessel. "Brain Sex" in *Behavioral Endocrinology*. Cambridge, MA: MIT Press/ Bradford Books. 1992.

John Laffin. *Brassey's Battles: 3500 Years of Conflict, Campaigns and Wars From A to Z*. London: A Wheaton and Co. 1986.

Larue, Gerald A. *Gero-Ethics*. Prometheus Books. 1992.

Leslie, Gerald R. and Sheila K. Korman. *The Family in Social Context*. Oxford Universit Press. New York, 1989.

Levant, Ronald F. "The New Psychology of Men." *Professional Psychology Research and Practice*. 1996. vol. 27. No.3.

Levinson, Daniel J. *The Seasons of a Man's Life*. Ballantine Books. NY. 1978.

de Lisser, Eleena. "For Inner-City Youth a Hard Life May Lead To a Hard Sentence." *Wall Street Journal*. Nov. 30, 1993. p. 1.

Malinowski, Bronislaw. *Sex, Culture and Myth.* New York: Harcourt, Brace and World. 1962.

Marcel, Gabriel. *The Decline of Wisdom.* Philosophical Library. New York. 1955.

Mathews, Mitford M. *A Dictionary of Americanism on Historical Principles.* University of Chicago Press, Chicago. vol.II.1951.

Mead, Margaret. *Culture and Commitment.* Natural History Press. New York. 1970

Mead, Margaret. *Male and Female.* New York. 1955.

Miller, Alice. *The Untouched Key: Tracing Childhood Trauma in Creativity and Destructiveness.* New York: Doubleday. 1990.

Minuchin, Salvador. *Families and Family Therapy.* Harvard University Press. Cambridge, Mass. 1974

Modell, John, Fran F. Furstenberg Jr. And Douglas Strong. "The Timing of Marriage In The Transition to Adulthood: Continuity and Change, 1860-1975 "*American Journal of Sociology.* vol. IV. 1978.

Moore, Robert and Gillette, Douglas. *King, Warrior, Magician, Lover.* HarperCollins Pub. San Francisco. 1990.

Myss, Caroline. *Anatomy of the Spirit.* New York. Harmony Books. 1996.

Palmer, Parker. *The Courage to Teach.* Jossey-Bass Inc. Pub. San Francisco. 1998

Parke, Ross D. *Fathers.* Cambridge: Harvard U. Press. 1981.

Pintauro, Joseph and Sister Corita. *To Believe in God.* Harper and Row Pub. New York. 1968.

Polanyi, Karl. *The Great Transformation.* Beacon Press. Boston. 1957.

Popenoe, David. *Life Without Fathers.* The Free Press. NY. 1996.

Plutarch. "Whether an Old Man Should Engage in Public Affairs?" Moralia. X. "Old Men in Public Affairs." 784. P.81. Quoted in *Minois. History of Old Age.*

"Preserving and Cherishing the Earth: An Appeal For Joint Commitment in Science and Religion." Moscow. 1991. Quoted in David Suzuki and Peter Knudtson. *Wisdom of the Elders*. Bantam Books. New York. 1992. P.227.

Rinpoche, Sogyal. *The Tibetan Book of Living and Dying*. Harper San Francisco. New York. 1994.

St. Jerome. Letters. p. 61. Letter XIV. Quoted in George Minois. *History of Old Age*. Un iversity of Chicago Press. 1987.

Schachter-Shalomi, Zalman. *Age-ing and Sage-ing*. Warner Books. N.Y. 1995.

Schor, Juliet B. *The Overworked American*. Harper Collins. New York.1992.

Silverstein, Olga and Beth Rashbaum. *The Courage to Raise Good Men*. Penguin Books. NY. 1994.

Simmons, Leo. *The Role of the Aged in Primitive Society*. New Haven. 1945.

Smalley, Gary and Trent, John. *Blessing*. Tape cassette. Pocket Books. 1990.

Susuki, David and Peter Knudtson. *Wisdom of the Elders*. Bantam Books. New York. 1992.

Taylor, A.E. *Socrates*. Doubleday: Garden City, NY. 1953.

Thoreau, Henry David. *Walden*. Signet Classics edition. 1980.

Turner, Frederick G. "Middle Western Pioneer Democracy."(1918*) The Frontier in American History*. Rinehart and Winston. 1962. New York.

U.S. Bureau of the Census. Current Population Reports. Series P-20. No. 467. (Wash. DC US Government Printing Office. April, 1993) XVI.

U.S. Dept. of Health and Human Services. Sept. 9, 1993.9,30. Advance Report of the Final Mortality Statistics, 1991. Vol. 42. No.3, Supplement, Monthly Vital Statistics Report. (Hyattsville, Md)

U.S. National Commission on Children. *Beyond Rhetoric*. Douglas J. Besharov, Testimony before the Select Committee on Children, Youth and Families. (Wash, DC. US Government Printing Office. 1987. pp. 32-33.

Van Gennep, Arnold. *The Rites of Passage*. Chicago. University of Chicago Press. 1960.

Wells, H.G. *The Outline of History*. vol. II. Garden City Books. New York. 1920.

Whitmont, E.C. *The Symbolic Quest*. Barrie and Rockliff: London. 1969.

Xenophon, "Memorabilia of Socrates," in Socratic Discourse Plato and Xenophon, Everyman's Library, London. 1910.

Zukav, Gary. *The Seat of the Soul*. Simon and Schuster. New York. 1989.

Back row, left to right: Joshua, Jason, Jeremy, Kirk
Front row, left to right: Caleb, Valentino, Terry, Joshua

ABOUT THE AUTHOR

Terry Jones is a psychotherapist, a spiritual director and president of EASE, Employee Assistance Services Enterprises, Inc., one of the oldest mental health consulting firms in the West. He received his MA in history from Sonoma State University, and his M.Ed. in counseling from Lewis and Clark College.

He has authored several works including a paperback, *Also of Men Born*. Terry is a public speaker and conducts seminars and workshops. Father of six and grandfather of five, Terry lives with his wife of thirty years in West Linn, Oregon.

To order additional copies of:

THE ELDER WITHIN

The Source of
Mature Masculinity

$16.95 US / $24.95 Canada
$4.50 Shipping & Handling

Contact:

B∞KPARTNERS
I N C O R P O R A T E D

P.O. Box 922
Wilsonville, OR 97070
Fax: 503-682-2057
Phone: 503-682-3235
E-mail: info@bookpartners.com